What people are sayin

PEACL

"Dr. Tajiri's book brings the reader intimately close to the challenges and life-changing journey of combat to transformative healing from the wounds of war. As a combat veteran with multiple deployments and extended times in the carnage of war, I heartily recommend this book to veterans, their loved ones, and those who seek to understand or join the healing journey with our veterans."

Dr. Roderick Mills, LtCol (Ret.) Army,
president of AeroNova Ministries, adjunct
professor at Regent University, senior fellow
of the Center for Transformational Living

"Powerful! As a person of faith, Dr. Tajiri applies her clinical training, her military experience as an officer, her walk with God, and her knowledge of Scripture to promote the healing of emotional and spiritual wounds that plague many of our military service personnel."

Robert Johnson, COL, PhD,
forensic neuropsychologist

"Taking on this topic requires bravery, and Dr. Tiffany demonstrates plenty. This book is a no-holds-barred approach to dealing with the effects of combat trauma. As a veteran (and now a licensed therapist myself) who has dealt with the impact of PTSD and the suicide of my fellow Soldiers, I am grateful for a book that is so direct.

Bobby Jackson, LCSW, pastoral coach, cofounder
of Rallypoint Ministry, author of Regroup
curriculum, former Army Soldier and medic

"Military chaplains must get their hands on this book and use it as a force multiplier for spiritual healing before and after combat. As a Chaplain and combat veteran, I have been touched by the freeing and uplifting insight in this book. Its real and gritty nature allows our loved ones to see the truth of what's brewing in our souls—yet instills hope through faith for a better tomorrow."

Soon Jung, MAJ (R), Army Chaplain,
6-9th Sqd, 9th US Cavalry

"Pastoring in El Paso, Texas, home to Fort Bliss and many Army heroes, I know firsthand the great need for the content in this book. Dr. Tajiri communicates her heart to help, along with profound wisdom and much-needed information. This book inspires and reminds us that hope and healing are possible!"

Shannon Nieman, lead pastor of Abundant
Church, founder of One Sisterhood

"Dr. Tajiri doesn't shy away from the gritty reality that gives birth to the gauntlet of fear, regret, and guilt of our returning warriors. She does a wonderful job of balancing science, Scripture, and warrior-speak in a welcoming approach that meets the Service Member where they currently are. I hope this book gets into the hands of every returning Service Member struggling to reconcile their faith with their deployed experiences and every family member struggling to understand them in turn.

Brett Banks, executive director of USO Alaska
(the opinion expressed is that of the endorser and not of the USO)

"*Peace after Combat* is a direct hit to the heart of the matter. In real time and authentic ways, Dr. Tajiri reaches in and accosts the racing thoughts and questions that suffocate our Service Members, veterans, and first responders. The promise to leave no man or woman behind is officially fulfilled amid these pages, among the hearts, souls, and bone marrow of our brothers and sisters who have answered the call."

Kristina Seymour, PsyD, Thriving psychologist, author, USAF Veteran, 1991–1995, wife of an Army Ranger (class of 12-93)

"Everyone knows that setbacks can happen in life. Unfortunately, most people do not have the skills, tools, and recourses to work through life's challenges. Dr. Tiffany has spent much of her life helping people work through difficult situations. In her new book, she gives incredible insight and tools to help us regain the life we were intended to live."

Tim Storey, acclaimed author, speaker, pastor, life coach

"As the South Texas regional director for the Birdwell Foundation for PTSD, I endorse without reluctance Dr. Tiffany Tajiri's phenomenal book *Peace after Combat*. Within this book lies the truth, remedy, and direction for our military, first responders, and those preparing to deploy. This book is the complete guidance you will need."

Mike Gonzales, CW3 (Ret.), Army, Military Occupational Skills 11B Infantry, 88M Platoon Sergeant, 882A Mobility Warrant Officer; Saudi Arabia 1997, Afghanistan 2002, Iraq 2004, 2009

"Dr. Tajiri eloquently weaves personal stories of combat trauma recovery with the redemptive healing power of our loving Savior. Her traditional clinical methods are complimented by spiritual truths helpful for all who are fighting their own inner battles. *Peace after Combat* is an inspirational guide for those who seek recovery and, ultimately, God's plan for their life."

Jon Allman, president & CEO of Endeavors

"Accurate! This is a book I would recommend to any combat veteran and military couple regardless of branch. Should be a part of every General's reading list."

Mijikai Mason, CH (MAJ), MDiv, MA Marriage
and Family Therapy, transitioning officer, Chaplain,
marriage counselor, author; Desert Shield/
Storm, OIF III, OIF V-VI, OEF 2012–2013

"Dr. Tajiri brings incredible insight toward helping and healing our hurting heroes. Her illustrations are real; the pain and darkness she deals with are genuine and destructive. Yet she does not back down from helping her patients—and all of us who desire to help the hurting—by focusing on real truths that bring light, healing, and restoration."

Charles Nieman, founder and senior pastor
of Abundant Living Faith Center

"Wow! Immediate connection from the start! Dr. Tiffany's words are the truth my husband lives every day, making it easier for him to share his story and speak about his once deeply buried emotions. It helped normalize our experiences as a couple and has brought new hope for continued healing through Jesus Christ."

Gina Montalbano, PhD educational
leadership, Army wife

"As a retired Army recruiter, I believe firmly that this book should be given to Soldiers early in their career. Soldiers need to go into deployment knowing that God is not the author of the destruction they may encounter. We must equip them to be resilient physically, mentally, and spiritually. Get this book into as many hands as possible."

Lloyd Parker, 1Sgt (Ret.), Operations
and Intelligence Air Defense,
Infantry, and Army Recruiting

"Leading a recovery ministry alongside Dr. Tiffany, I have seen firsthand the incredible breakthroughs achieved using Rhythm Restoration. This book blends science and faith in a way I have never seen before. I can only imagine how liberating it will be for so many men and women to learn that they can be free and enjoy life again."

Jimmy Salas, executive pastor, Abundant Church

"Peace after Combat is a refreshing addition to the body of literature currently available dealing with PTSD. Dr. Tajiri acknowledges that science is of God and not in conflict with Him. Any true healing must be based on relationship with the Lord. She offers hope for healing and reconciliation for anyone who struggles with PTSD."

James C. Harbridge, LTC (Ret.) Army, field
staff with Officers' Christian Fellowship

"After reading the book, we both felt as though we were better equipped to provide mentoring for fellow veterans wherever we meet them. Moreover, the book helped us understand our military experiences in a new context—embedded in faith and love."

Jeffrey (Jeff) J. Pickard, COL (Ret.),
USAF, and **Heather E. Pickard,** USAF
veteran, Key Spouse mentor

"This book is a must for the returning veteran struggling to cope with the imbalances of reconciling violent and dramatic combat episodes with loved ones who see drastic change yet want to help, but don't know how. Recommended!"

Kurt Ebaugh, LtCol, USMC
(Ret.), Iraq War Veteran

"Dr. Tiffany shares proven ideas and real-life success stories that are missing in our leader and family member training. A must-read that will enlighten leaders at all levels who are preparing their units, Service Members, and families for deployment and, ultimately, a successful post-deployment reintegration."

Mike Harris, COL (Ret.), former Army commander, 6/8 Cavalry Squadron, and **Angie Harris**

"After reading Dr. Tiffany Tajiri words, I understand more intensely the Soldiers' pain and feel their suffering and struggles to keep going. This book has brought me through to another level in my own spiritual world and a greater need to follow faith."

Nanette West, Gold Star Mother

"*Peace after Combat* captures the warrior spirit of our US Armed Forces. Dr. Tiffany illustrates that God not only provides the strength and spirit to overcome battle and great adversity, but He will also provide the strength and spirit for healing and recovery. This book provides a clear pathway forward for military members, veterans, and their families."

Scott Graves, MAJ USAF pilot and Capt **Andrea Graves,** PsyD, clinical psychologist, USAF

PEACE

AFTER

COMBAT

DR TIFFANY TAJIRI

PEACE

AFTER

COMBAT

HEALING THE SPIRITUAL & PSYCHOLOGICAL WOUNDS OF WAR

DAVID C COOK

transforming lives together

PEACE AFTER COMBAT
Published by David C Cook
4050 Lee Vance Drive
Colorado Springs, CO 80918 U.S.A.

Integrity Music Limited, a Division of David C Cook
Brighton, East Sussex BN1 2RE, England

The graphic circle C logo is a registered trademark of David C Cook.

To protect the privacy of our combat veterans, the stories in this book use fictional characters whose experiences and emotional reactions accurately reflect their struggles.

Unless otherwise noted, all Scripture quotations are taken from the Holy Bible, New International Version®, NIV®. Copyright © 1973, 2011 by Biblica, Inc.™ Used by permission of Zondervan. All rights reserved worldwide. www.zondervan.com. The "NIV" and "New International Version" are trademarks registered in the United States Patent and Trademark Office by Biblica, Inc.™ Scripture quotations marked ESV are taken from the ESV® Bible (The Holy Bible, English Standard Version®), copyright © 2001 by Crossway, a publishing ministry of Good News Publishers. Used by permission. All rights reserved; MSG are taken from THE MESSAGE, copyright © 1993, 20018 by Eugene H. Peterson. Used by permission of NavPress, represented by Tyndale House Publishers. All rights reserved; NASB are taken from the (NASB®) New American Standard Bible®, Copyright © 1960, 2020 by The Lockman Foundation. Used by permission. All rights reserved. www.lockman.org; NKJV are taken from the New King James Version®. Copyright © 1982 by Thomas Nelson. Used by permission. All rights reserved; NLT are taken from the Holy Bible, New Living Translation, copyright © 1996, 2015 by Tyndale House Foundation. Used by permission of Tyndale House Publishers, Inc., Carol Stream, Illinois 60188. All rights reserved.

Library of Congress Control Number 2021932376
ISBN 978-0-8307-8195-9
eISBN 978-0-8307-8196-6

© 2021 Tiffany N. Tajiri

Rhythm Restoration™ is in process of being registered as a
trademark by Tiffany Tajiri. All rights reserved.

The Team: Michael Covington, Stephanie Bennett, Judy Gillispie, Leigh Davidson, James Hershberger, Angie Messinger, Susan Murdock
Cover Design: James Hershberger
Cover Photo: Getty Images

Printed in the United States of America
First Edition 2021

1 2 3 4 5 6 7 8 9 10

041621

This book is dedicated to my fellow warriors for their selfless service to protect and preserve our nation under God. It is with the greatest reverence that I give you my deepest appreciation, as I truly understand that freedom isn't free. Your service to our country came at a cost; you didn't have to do it, but you did it anyway. In the name of Jesus, it is my hope that you come to understand just how precious your sacrifice truly is.

CONTENTS

FOREWORD

As I enter the large building with my party, I realize this door is also the only exit. The further I proceed into the building, the more I sense the disadvantage I'll be at in order to get out safely. And then, as I maneuver around a corridor within said building, I also realize there are barriers and shelves on either side that degrade my peripheral vision. The noise of unknown people behind me, coupled with a sideways, wheeled obstacle blocking the aisle in front of me, further puts me in a perceived fatal funnel. My heart rate rises and I begin to sweat as I look to get myself out of this supposed vulnerable position and find safer ground. I look for dominant areas to position myself so that I have eyes on everyone and my six is secure. I speed up or slow down my movement to maintain freedom to maneuver. I am on constant alert until I finally exit the same doorway I entered and the fresh air and distance provide me greater comfort and safety. Where was I? I was not back in combat in Iraq or Afghanistan; I was in my local grocery store. The spiritual and psychological wounds of war are real, and what I just described is a normal reaction at home to the abnormal circumstances experienced in combat.

I served in the United States Army for almost thirty-eight years. My career culminated with my duty as the Senior Enlisted Advisor to the Chairman of the Joint Chiefs of Staff, the senior noncommissioned officer in the United States military. During my years of service, I participated in five combat tours of duty, including the combat parachute assault into Panama during Operation Just Cause, Operation Desert Storm, two tours in Operation Iraqi Freedom, and Operation Enduring

Freedom in Afghanistan. Countless times I experienced the sting of enemy fire amid numerous firefights and witnessed firsthand the cost of war in the loss and maiming of American Service Members. Although I was in denial for decades, only recently did I finally come to grips with my own PTSD and begin to confront my personal hidden wounds of war by entering therapy. It was the best decision I have ever made.

I met Dr. Tiffany through a colleague I served with during the surge in Iraq in 2007. I first read a draft of her book on a business flight home. As I began to immerse myself in the reading, memories of my five combat tours became more vivid and I became emotional right there in front of my fellow passengers. I saw myself in some of the characters within the draft. The hypervigilance, grief, and fear from my traumatic combat experiences and from losing so many good men and women were laid out before me in Dr. Tiffany's writing. She provides an accurate account of what the psychological wounds of war can do to the combat veteran and also to their family. In addition, she provides solutions that include faith, therapy, and activity to assist the warrior in truly being able to mentally and emotionally come home.

I highly recommend this book to anyone with past combat service, their families, and our current uniformed warriors and their families. This book will provide the reader with a great description of how the unseen wounds of a warrior can adversely affect Service Members and their families. Most important, the material will show that conditions like posttraumatic stress disorder, depression, and anxiety are treatable and that the Service Member can not only learn coping skills to lead a normal life but truly attain peace after combat!

John Wayne Troxell
Department of Defense, Senior Enlisted Advisor
to the Chairman (Retired), US Army

PREFACE

Dear Combat Veteran,

Welcome home. You must be feeling overwhelmed right now. Perhaps even strangely disappointed?

Returning home isn't all it's cracked up to be. The pomp and circumstance are lackluster. The cheering crowds and smothering hugs make you want to jump out of your skin.

You're confused. Your family expects you to act and feel a certain way, and you're not having it. But you try anyway, terrified you'll let them down. How can your wife, husband, or children be so physically near and yet so emotionally distant? They're starting to notice your fake smile.

You don't understand why you want to go back to "hell." How can being here, on US soil, feel so foreign and complicated? Maybe this wasn't your first deployment. Maybe you and your family already know the routine and are struggling with it again—feeling more and more disconnected with each of your returns.

Believe it or not, what you're experiencing is common—it's just that no one talks about it. Take a breath … and know that it will get better. But improving your current emotional state will not result from a passive process of avoidance but rather an active one that will require spiritual and psychological fortitude.

For the past year or so of deployment, you lived with a constant target on your head. What you saw may have radically changed how you view yourself, others, and the world around you. You may never have seen so much hurt, suffering, death, and destruction in your life. At some point in the middle of it all, you may have asked, "Where is God?"

Your beliefs about your experiences may cause you to lose sleep at night and may relentlessly punish you by day. Slowly this mindset eats away at your faith as you look for where to place the blame. Some days you blame yourself and other days you blame God.

Why don't you feel like the hero that America props you up to be? Some say they feel more like monsters for the things they did—or didn't do—while in combat. Civilians don't understand—creating a greater divide between them and us.

You bear a painful burden for this country that only you and those who fought beside you truly understand.

If any of this sounds familiar, please keep reading. Let the words of this book help you unravel your painful beliefs so you can finally experience peace. You're not alone.

Very Respectfully,
Dr. Tiffany Tajiri, USAF Veteran

INTRODUCTION

*They died and it's my fault. I can't close
my eyes without seeing their faces. I'm not
a hero; I'm a monster. If you only knew....
Where was God? Is He punishing me?*
—Active duty Soldier

*Whoever dwells in the shelter of the Most
High will rest in the shadow of the Almighty.
I will say of the LORD, "He is my refuge and
my fortress, my God, in whom I trust."*
—Psalm 91:1–2

Is it possible to find peace after returning from combat? One US combat veteran dies by suicide every hour. Over 90 percent of our combat veterans profess a belief in God and goodness, but many of them lose their faith after experiencing the horrors of war. Even if they can somehow hold on to their faith, many insist that their combat sins will only send them to hell. Such flawed and tragic beliefs make it easier to consider suicide.

After each traumatic deployment, combat veterans are dramatically less inclined to believe. Faith and family are the strongest protective factors in suicide prevention, but often families fail because of the strain deployments place on marriages. All that's left is faith, but what happens when faith is seemingly lost?

The purpose of my book is to assure you that faith cannot and will not fail you. In fact, it is faith that will bring an unexplainable peace to your life and those you love.

Let me remind you of the truth that sets you free:

- God understands you, never left you, loves you, forgives you, and will do anything to have a relationship with you.
- God is not the author of your hurt and suffering. He is not the author of the terrible things you saw in combat.
- Every day we are engaged in spiritual warfare, and whether the battlefield is in the Sandbox (Middle East) or in our heads, we cannot succumb to the Enemy (Satan), who wants us to lose sight of God.

Have you ever stopped to think about how much you are like Christ? Yes, you read that right—Jesus Christ—as in *the* Son of God! Just as Jesus selflessly sacrificed His life for our eternal salvation, you (and of course, those lost along the way) volunteered to sacrifice your life for God and country. As you know, freedom isn't free. The Bible tells us "there is no greater love than to lay down one's life for one's friends" (John 15:13 NLT).

Jesus wasn't immune to experiencing the hurt and pain caused by our world. In fact, He completely understands your suffering, as everything pales in comparison to what He endured during His life and finally His death on the cross.

Jesus never abandoned you and your brothers and sisters whom you lost in combat; He was always there.

I pray that you do not succumb to the lies of the Enemy: lies of self-blame, lies of shame, lies about God not loving you, lies about God punishing you, lies about your life never getting any better, lies about being unworthy, and even worse.

Spiritual warfare is as real as you and me. Don't forget that you are called to be a warrior of the flesh *and* of the spirit. Now it's time to fight for your life and take back everything the Enemy has stolen. You're not alone. God is on your side and the victory is already yours—you just need to fight for it. Let's put on that battle rattle and press on.

> Put on the full armor of God, so that you can take your stand against the devil's schemes. For our struggle is not against flesh and blood, but against the rulers, against the authorities, against the powers of this dark world and against the spiritual forces of evil in the heavenly realms. (Eph. 6:11–12)

Before we go any further, you may be wondering who I am and why you should trust a word I have to share with you. You're right to ask, and I respect your skepticism. You don't have the benefit of meeting me face to face like many of those whom I counsel. When I meet a combat veteran at his or her first session, I'm typically greeted with an expression of surprise. I'm petite and I look young for my age.

"Hello. I'm Dr. Tiffany." I'll smile and firmly shake his hand with an intent gaze.

"Hi," he'll grumble back and shift in his seat.

After we spend a minute reviewing my well-scripted limits of confidentiality, I'll ask for permission to speak about myself so he'll see me as a real person—not just as a sterile, know-it-all psychotherapist. I'll share some facts about my life with him.

I'll maintain eye contact, but his eyes will quickly and diligently scan the room as if he is on a patrol.

"You were military?" he'll ask.

"Yes. You're very observant—not a surprise." The military in me acknowledges the military in him. In that moment, the ice begins to defrost.

I'll hand him the picture he's noticed from my desk for a closer look, allowing him to ascertain the time, place, and situation. It shows me standing on a beach in Florida with my battle uniform covered in mud and sand after rucking with Special Forces.

"Do you miss it?" he may ask.

"Of course, but I'll live it again very soon," I say confidently.

"How?" He puts the pieces together in his head, calculating every breath of interaction between us. It didn't make sense to him when I told him that I left the military for the stable life of raising my son with my husband in my hometown.

"I'll live it again, but this time through your eyes."

And we begin.

Part I

Understanding Combat Experiences

*Why we feel this way and where God
is in the midst of our suffering*

Chapter 1

POSTTRAUMATIC STRESS

Welcome Home, Hero!

James's Story (US Marine)

It's been two weeks since I've returned from Afghanistan. I don't know what to f***in' do with myself. I'm wound so tight that I'd rather be back there. It doesn't make sense to feel the way I do right now—in my own home, no less. Is everyone else living it up on leave but me? What the f***?

My sweaty a** is stuck to this old, worn-out couch. I'm irritated at everything. My wife sits with her arms crossed and a scowl across her face. She's pissed at me—at everything I do and don't do. She's been waiting for me to be extra lovey-dovey to make up for my absence. F*** that! I'll jump out of my skin if I do that. I want to smother all of them in my love, but I have none to give. I'm f***in' empty.

The kids are playing on the floor—between us and the television. The baby is in the bouncer, and the two tots are preoccupied on iPads. I'll give them anything to shut up right now, but then Cole sees something on Tia's screen and yanks the iPad from her. Tia pitches a bloody fit, and Cole follows suit.

My body reflexively flies off the couch and into a yelling rage. "You either need to shut up or go to your rooms." I walk briskly out onto the back porch. From the corner of my eye, I see my wife swoop down to

scoop up the two tots. She glares at me through the sliding glass doors.
Even from outside I hear the kids sniffling, and that's even more f***in'
irritating. I open my third and final pack of smokes for the evening.
Back and forth, I pace the patio's perimeter.

"Hey, Marine! Who the f*** do you think you are coming home
and disrupting everything I had in order?" my wife shouts out as she
steps onto the patio.

"You call this f***in' order?" I kick the dog sh** lying at the edge
of the patio.

She slams the door shut and returns to soothing the baby's hella-
cious screams. Even from the distance of the backyard, with the screams
muted, the sound of that child makes my skin crawl.

A thin film of sweat instantly appears on my body. My feet refuse
to keep pacing. I close my eyes and—*flashback*—I'm right back in a
f***in' house raid. Screaming babies, children, and mothers—all
running chaotically through the home. I can't pull myself from that
moment. In the middle of the raid, this woman handed me her screaming baby and ran away. I don't f***in' understand what possessed her to
do that. I'll never forget the distress on the tiny creature's face. I reached
to hand his wailing body off to some boy, and he ripped the baby from
my arms in terror and anger. He stared at me for an instant with a look
of absolute disgust. *At that moment, I realized I was a real-life monster.*

I walk to the edge of the backyard and slam my fist into the rock
wall. Pain is the only distraction from this moment. I welcome the
sensation as it courses through my arm and down my back. I smash
my fist into the wall—again and again. There's relief in watching the
cement stone burst into a gray cloud and crumble to the ground. The
blood from my knuckles drips onto the earth, a combination of sparse
grass and sand.

Instantly, my mind shifts to the memory of Mark's last breath. Like a projector, my brain casts the image of his blood spreading through the white sand and me shoveling fresh sand to cover it. We never left evidence of our defeat; the enemy would never gain that satisfaction. *It's my fault he died; I should've seen that IED.* I throw my fist into the wall again.

My face burns from the salty tears that break free. I wipe my face with the bottom of my shirt. As I make my way back to the house, I kick another portion of the constellation of dried dog sh** in my path.

My wife tries to make eye contact through the kitchen window, but I don't give her the time of day. I know she cares, but after two weeks she's already too f***in' fed up with me. I walk into the kitchen and a loud sigh escapes from her. "Shut up," I reply. Another guttural sigh erupts from her. F*** it. It's not worth my breath.

I open the fridge and reach to pull out my third six-pack for the day. Everything in threes (my lucky number that kept me alive). As I'm leaning for the beer bottle at the bottom of the fridge—F***! My body instinctively collapses into a fetal position on the ground, hands tucked behind my head.

"Get up!" she yells at me. "It's just the damn garbage disposal."

My heart races, and all of a sudden, I'm nothing. I'm weak. I'm a coward. I hate myself. The fact that she saw me crumble like a leaf sends a flood of embarrassment and vulnerability straight through me. F*** *that* feeling. The weakness turns to anger, and I direct a slew of curse words that rip through her, causing her to drop the plate she's washing onto the floor. The sound of the crashing causes me to flinch—again. She looks down at the mess and up at me with a look of pure disgust. I'm that f***in' monster again. Perhaps I've always been a monster—and always will be.

I put three beers in my oversized shirt, grab a fourth as I zip past the kids, and head straight for the garage. I fling the door wide open and stumble over the air mattress, losing a beer in the process. It hits and explodes all over the floor, the sound sending another shockwave through me. F*** it! After I recover my balance, I reach for the bottle opener on the workbench. The pop and fizz sounds send excitement through my body, signaling that relief will follow.

The beer burns going down, but I don't stop chugging. I pause for a moment to let the carbonation settle before I open the second bottle. I feel like a guilty drunk, but I don't care enough to stop. F*** it! The elation from opening the third bottle isn't quite as strong, but it's still a rush. I can use any rush I can get. *Chug, chug, chug, chug …* I repeat the word in my mind like a frat boy at a college party. *Did I miss out by not going to college? Did I make a mistake joining the military?* Who gives a sh**. At this point, it doesn't f***in' matter.

I fall backward onto my air mattress. The acid from the beer rises into my esophagus and burns. Everything f***ing burns. Welcome home, hero! Blood rushes to my brain and the buzz starts to catch. The broken bottle is just feet from the mattress. Broken. I'm broken. Just like that beer, there's nothing left of me to salvage.

I close my eyes and open them immediately. Closing them is like watching a movie reel of every deployment experience gone wrong. It's torture—my own personal hell. Perhaps I deserve it. I can't sleep and I feel like I'm going crazy. No—I've already gone crazy.

I'm a burden to my family. It was easier for them when I was gone. I turn in the direction of the safe on the wall where I keep my gun. It would be so much easier for all of us if I did it. Jake did it; I can too. My family would get hundreds of thousands of dollars of life insurance. Veronica can remarry a nice man who can be the good type of father my kids need and deserve. Almost any guy is better than me.

My body feels like a deadweight as I roll off the mattress to my knees. I take a knee. F*** that! I've taken one too many knees. I don't want to feel that emotional pain. I've taken a knee over six dead bodies on this deployment. I stand too quickly and sway to catch my balance.

I walk across the garage and reach for the safe. I still remember the code. It's a sign! Inside the safe lies my freedom—the only way out of my torment. I breathe a sigh of relief. My handgun is locked and loaded, ready to go—another sign! I rush back to the mattress and climb under a blanket. I'm not going to make a mess all over the garage. I'll keep it contained for Veronica's sake, though she might enjoy the sight of me dead—a relief for her as well. The alcohol and cigarette buzz swarms through my body in a pleasant tingle. For about a minute, I stop to enjoy this last sensation of being alive.

God, if I was fighting for Your good cause, why do I feel like this? Why do You allow me to feel like this? Why haven't You stopped it? I don't understand. You don't understand. But if I'm meant to die like this, I will. God, forgive me, if You even exist.

God, if I was fighting for Your good cause, why do I feel like this?

I open my mouth and quickly slip the gun in—not mindful of the process. To do this, there is no room for hesitation. My hands adjust around the trigger and pistol as I wiggle myself into the center of the mattress to ensure that my body cannot be seen. Veronica will hear the gunshot, run into the garage, and walk in on a small stream of blood dripping from the mattress—clean and neat—not like the sh** I saw in Afghanistan. Let's do this. I close my eyes and slowly draw in my last breath.

"Daddy. Da-da. Ready or not, here we come!" Cole shouts as he and his sister barge through the garage door.

F***. Their time-out is over. I hide the gun under the covers and pop up from the mattress. "Boo!" I shout as I run to chase my children out into the yard.

I need help. God, help me! Please![†]

☆ ☆ ☆

If James's experience sounds all too familiar, then it's time to understand why you're feeling the way you do. Your experience is more common than you may think. No one talks about it because no one wants to be perceived as weak. It takes courage to admit that you're not who you were before you deployed or who you want to be now. The good news is that there are scientific and spiritual reasons to explain what you're going through now. When you learn the whys behind how you're feeling, you'll begin to find peace for the first time in a long time.

Here's the BLUF (bottom line up front): most people will not use the words *spiritual* and *psychological* in the same sentence, as many believe that God and science cannot coexist. Yet the subtitle of this book pairs these words together.

It's simple: God created mankind in His image (see Gen. 1:27), and He created us using science. We are a series of biochemical reactions, each equipped with a personality and a slew of emotions—many of which are godly emotions. The primary characteristic of God's very being is *love* (see 1 John 4:8). Our purpose as created beings is to love

---

†   Emotional and physical abuse of any person is wrong. If you find yourself prone to this sort of aggressive behavior, please seek help immediately.

and be loved; we are neurobiologically wired to do so. That being said, the love within us is from God, and how it makes us feel is derived by science, the mechanism of action God used to create us. You can't separate God and science, so stop trying.

Research has proven time and time again that when a person has faith, he or she is significantly more resilient and psychologically capable of overcoming hurtful experiences. Faith provides us with deep meaning and a productive purpose for everything we encounter in our lives. You are a spiritual being in a human body.

There are significant differences in the neurophysiology of the brains of individuals who have strong faith versus no faith. Dr. Lisa Miller describes a cortical thickening in the parietal cortex that is observed in the brains of spiritual persons—contributing to neuro-protective benefits. More specifically, she states that those individuals with a spiritual life are 80 percent less likely to experience depression.[‡]

In this chapter, I will focus primarily on the science of your brain and why you feel the way you feel, only dipping our toes in the waters of spirituality. In later chapters, we will plunge deeper into that water.

Like a Shrapnel Wound

There are all sorts of opinions regarding what defines a traumatic experience. Sometimes psychobabble definitions sound too theoretical, so let's make it more concrete. For the purpose of this book, a traumatic experience is any event that causes us intense psychological distress, so much so that it jumbles our view of ourselves, the world, and our spiritual belief system. Such a traumatic event keeps us stuck in a pattern of unhealthy thinking, feeling, and behaving.

Imagine that your arm caught shrapnel from an exploded IED. The doc wraps it up for you, and you keep charging on, no time to stop.

‡   Lisa Miller, *The Spiritual Child* (New York: Picador, 2016).

The wound may eventually become infected, and it may begin to cause you pain when you sleep on it. But finally, it closes. It looks awful and it hurts, but there's no chance to address it now. You have to stay in the fight at all costs. You reason that it's best to treat the infected wound upon your return from deployment.

Now that you're home, it's time to get that wound looked at. Your doctor tells you that it's infected and he or she needs to cut it open and drain out all the bacteria. This is the only way to remove the infection and allow it to heal properly. The process is painful, and the healing is uncomfortable, but it's worth it to be able to someday sleep on it again without pain. Of course, you'll be left with a scar, but that doesn't matter because you'll be healed and pain-free.

Similarly, the psychological processing of trauma causes us to hurt again when we reopen the emotional wound we acquired on the battle-field. Just like the physical wound, the emotional wound takes time to heal. The healing process of the physical wound was interrupted by a bacterial infection, while the healing process of the emotional wound was interrupted by toxic thinking patterns like shame and twisted guilt (to be discussed). Make sense?

If you were physically wounded in combat, don't be surprised if it takes significantly longer to heal from the emotional side effects of your injury. Of course, the severity and permanence of a physical wound make a difference. If you've permanently lost a physical function, such as sight or the ability to move freely due to the loss of a limb, you will have to grieve this loss. Such a loss can be similar to grieving the death of one of your nearest and dearest loved ones. Many survivors of such profound injuries heal more effectively when they find purpose in their losses and use their testimonies of overcoming to inspire others during similar hardships.

Even though you may never fully heal from your physical injury, the good news is that you are absolutely capable of healing your mind.

As it heals, your mind will be stretched to new dimensions from the experiences and understanding you gain. This is a good thing! I strongly believe the process of overcoming the traumatic events of our past equips us with so much knowledge of our thoughts, emotions, and behaviors that it makes us more in tune with ourselves and others. Once you have achieved this, you may consider yourself the recipient of an honorary doctorate in self-reflection. *"Let us examine our ways and test them, and let us return to the LORD"* (Lam. 3:40).

Shame: The Enemy's Superpower

An enemy out to destroy you is a familiar concept. Whether it's the physical enemy (Taliban, insurgents, ISIS, etc.) in the Sandbox, or the spiritual Enemy in your mind, the agenda is the same: your destruction on the battlefield. Shame is the Enemy's favorite weapon because it wrecks you from the inside out. The scary thing is that shame magnifies when you return home, and it attacks you in your most precious and vulnerable space: your heart and family.

Shame is the biggest liar! Shame causes you to feel unworthy of love and connection to God or anyone else. It tells you that no one could possibly love you if they truly knew you. Shame tells you that no one could possibly understand because you're crazy. It tells you anything and everything to keep you stuck in its black hole.

The Enemy's plan to attack your life purpose is brilliant. Shame forces you into isolation, which leads to depression and a downward spiral of emotional darkness. It feels impossible to escape! But did you know that God neurobiologically wired you to love and be loved? Here's the truth:

- you are worthy,
- you are deserving,
- you are lovable,

- you're not alone,
- others feel like you do,
- and you are profoundly loved!

Don't let the Enemy get you down before we've even begun.

Conquering shame requires us to have the courage to temporarily sit with the discomfort of vulnerability, admitting that we're not where we want to be emotionally or spiritually. If you can get past vulnerability, there is a place of love, growth, and healing. But our fear of vulnerability is the Devil whispering in our ears to quit, just when we've built up enough courage to take the huge step needed to turn our lives around. In the name of Jesus, let's break through together with open hearts and minds.

James will have to confront his shame and vulnerability head-on in order to experience psychological healing and improve his relationships with his wife and children. As treatment progresses, he will be more patient and less aggressive and begin to again feel emotionally connected to his loved ones. James will better understand his wife and have empathy and appreciation for her sacrifices and her patience with his past behaviors. But remember, a natural part of healing is that sometimes it can get worse (short-lived) before it gets better. It's important that your loved ones understand what you will be enduring when you begin treatment.

The Brain and the Gut

To better understand how your brain functions, it can help to compare its similarities to how your gut functions. Let's say you decide to take a chance on your local hole-in-the-wall Mexican restaurant. The prices are cheap, and the margarita glasses are never empty. You order the spiciest chicken enchiladas, and when they arrive, everything is covered in a greasy layer of cheese. *It's all good,* you think. *It can't be worse than living on MREs* (Meals, Ready-to-Eat) *for days on end.* You practically inhale the entire plate in less than five minutes. Then you wash it all down with a margarita pitcher and toss in salty tortilla chips with flaming hot salsa. You're young; your gut is made of steel, right? That night you don't leave the bathroom—you either experience an explosive toilet episode or constipation.

Your stomach delights in healthy meals, extracting and digesting the nutrients from the food to deliver to your whole body and then dumping the rest. But this particular meal was not entirely healthy! Turns out, that Mexican meal was a traumatic event for your gut. In the moment of consumption, it wasn't too painful, but hours later your gut shut down and rejected the unhealthy food.

Your brain must emotionally digest your life experiences. Information you obtain from your experiences is either retained and filed away in your long-term memory or it's dumped if it's not needed. When a traumatic event happens, your brain may experience "indigestion"—much like your gut. We can work through our brain indigestion when we process an event to make sense of it; we dissect what happened through examining our thoughts, emotions, and behaviors in light of our spiritual belief system. Why would our brain stop digesting an event? Because it's so unpleasant we want to avoid it! Avoidance is the hallmark symptom of posttraumatic stress. You may ask, "Can't we just keep the painful past in the past?" No! Because your past is the reason for your current symptom presentation.

How can we process a traumatic experience? We need to stop avoiding the subject and talk about it. We need to recall the experience, examine it, and make sense of it in our own minds. This may include asking how it fits with the rest of our worldview and our belief in God. When our thoughts, emotions, behaviors, and experiences do not flow in the same direction, our way of thinking becomes twisted, which leads to anxiety. Many times, we can become stuck in these thought patterns that inhibit (or constipate) the smooth processing of trauma. Twisted thinking is irrational and focuses on guilt, causing us to falsely believe we can control the world around us. (In upcoming chapters, we'll learn we don't control external events—only influence them.) Overcoming this unhealthy and illogical thought process is more than half the battle when trying to achieve peace of mind and digest our traumatic life experiences.

When a traumatic event happens,

your brain may experience

"indigestion"—much like your gut.

Here's an example of attempting to process a traumatic event. You believe God doesn't allow bad things to happen to good people (thought), you love God (emotion), you pray to God for safety (behavior), but then you get blown up on the battlefield (experience). Every thought, emotion, and behavior was congruent (in the same direction) in that scenario, but your experience was not. How do you process that? You may think you need to change your spiritual worldview to fit your experience. Instead you may need to be reminded that God does not will bad things but that all bad comes from the selfish decisions of others—essentially free will. This understanding will bring you the peace of continuing to believe in a good God but seeing how the selfish free will of others can have negative influence on people's lives.

James needs to emotionally digest and process the traumatic events that happened to him on deployment—from his brothers who died on the battlefield to the locals who viewed him as a monster. James is stuck on self-blame, shame, guilt, and anger. Moreover, he has shunned his relationship with God—resenting Him for all the tragedy he experienced in combat.

Fight, Flight, or Freeze Reaction

When your mind registers that you're in danger, it sends a signal to pump all the blood from your gut to your outer extremities: your arms and legs. This aids you in running or fighting for your survival. Additionally, your brain is hyperstimulated by adrenaline, which can either radically improve your performance on the battlefield or destroy it. During field training, you repeated tactical maneuvers hundreds of times, allowing your brain to go on autopilot and execute like a champion. Without training, you might still perform well, but you might also stall (freeze) in the middle of the battlefield. The practice and experience of field training exercises are designed to save the lives of you and your squad while in the Sandbox and also mute the conscious awareness of pain.

While in a war zone, your sympathetic nervous system (the part of the brain that triggers the fight-flight-freeze response) is always on high alert as a survival mechanism. The problem occurs when you maintain this sense of being "on guard," or hypervigilance, when you return to garrison (the United States).

Picture the Yugo, what some claim to be the "worst" car in the world. If you live in a windy city like me, the flimsy Yugo's theft alert system would go off every minute as an overreaction to a mere gust of wind. Unfortunately, you may be feeling like a Yugo, overreacting to normal stressors. You need to recalibrate your alert system. While on deployment, your alert system should be placed on "extreme sensitivity." But while in garrison, it should be readjusted to "mild-moderate sensitivity." Maintaining "extreme sensitivity" mode while in garrison will increase your levels of stress hormones (cortisol), exhausting your body and mind and making you more prone to illness.

James took cover when he heard the garbage disposal—a familiar, albeit loud, sound at home. James's alert system is hypersensitive and needs to be recalibrated to match his current level of threat. James combatted his hypervigilance (extreme alertness) by consuming a depressant: alcohol. He self-medicated with alcohol to reduce his stress threshold and to numb his negative thoughts and emotions caused by his intrusive deployment memories.

Triggers

When your brain registers a sensory experience (sight, sound, smell, taste, touch) similar to a traumatic life event, it will reflexively send you into the fight-or-flight reaction. You could be enjoying a picnic with your family until fireworks go off. The sensory stimulus of their flash, sound, and smell might then remind you of the traumatic event of being hit by an RPG. It could be a conscious (aware of) or subconscious (not aware of) reaction to the triggering stimulus. This may seem like an overreaction by your body, but it's a survival mechanism. Your brain clings tightly to memories that elicit powerful emotions such as fear. If the smell of burning tires was present when your life was at imminent risk, your brain will code the smell of burning tires as a threat to your safety.

No one wants to be sent into the flight-or-fight mode during an ordinary day that presents no threat to survival. Hence, we avoid things that trigger us. For many, the crowds of a superstore are a huge trigger because in a war zone, crowds pose a threat. Your brain remembers the time the suicide bomber exploded in a marketplace in Afghanistan.

If we spend our lives trying to avoid our triggers, we will eventually become hermits and never leave our homes. Our fear can become so overwhelming that in time, we may be too terrified to step outside to check the mailbox. Naturally, the more you avoid, the more of a problem it will pose for you long term.

The screams and cries of James's children triggered his memory of raiding a home in search of high-value targets (HVTs). James recognized that being in the presence of his crying baby would trigger him—sending him into a terrifying flashback (the short-lived feeling that one is reexperiencing the traumatic event). He experienced tremendous guilt for avoiding his own children.

Avoidance

Do you want to be reminded of your worst deployment experiences? Of course not! Most of us tend to suppress and avoid these traumatic memories at all costs. But your brain doesn't like that, and it does everything in its power to not allow that. Instead, the brain causes intrusive memories to pop up out of the blue, which is an awful distraction—almost impossible to shake off. The brain also insists on bringing up awful experiences in recurring nightmares. Why is your brain torturing you? Your brain isn't a procrastinator, even though you might be. This is a proactive attempt to force you to confront the issue and make sense of it—so your brain can file it away—and finally be at peace. In contrast, your continued avoidance is going against your brain's attempt to heal. You will never digest the traumatic experiences by avoiding them.

Here's another visual for you. Imagine you're a lazy cleaner (like me), and you decide to just sweep the dust and dirt under your favorite area rug. Avoiding the mess because you're too busy works for a while, but then one day, your dog takes a huge dump on that beautiful rug. In this analogy, the dump is equivalent to a traumatic life event. This pile cannot just be picked up. To salvage the lovely rug, you need to power wash it. As you lift up the corner to drag it outside, you're now forced to address not only the dog poop, but all the dirt you had swept under it. Similarly, one large traumatic event will trigger all the past, unprocessed emotional experiences you refused to psychologically "digest."

James used alcohol to avoid the toxic thoughts related to traumatic events he experienced on deployment. The alcohol helped to numb his suffering. Unbeknownst to him, it only worsened his guilt, insecurity, shame, and anger. Prior to his deployment, James had a history of childhood abuse and neglect. These unresolved childhood issues began to resurface along with his posttraumatic stress.

Congested Emotion

After a long family separation due to deployment, your emotions may feel confused or stunted. You may wonder why you feel emotionally disconnected from your loved ones in one moment or alternately find yourself being overwhelmed by their love and affections to the point that you need to distance yourself. Isolating is a double-edged sword. In the moment, it may feel like it's the only option that will maintain your sanity, but then you feel guilty for doing it. Why is it so hard to feel the right emotion, or any sort of emotion, even for those you love?

Think of your brain like an emotional hard drive that has reached its storage capacity. The emotional storage unit in your brain is called the limbic system. Inside this is the amygdala, the fear center of your brain, which stores all your traumatic life events. Because of what you've experienced, your fear center is full, it has overflowed into the rest of your emotional storage, and now that's full! Your ability to process emotion is shut down and no more emotional data can fit. The whole system needs to be organized and compressed to make additional space. Confront the issue and make some space!

Don't be surprised if you're forgetting things too. Your hippocampus, the part of the brain responsible for memory, is smack-dab in the middle of your limbic system. Since your limbic system has reached full storage capacity, your hippocampus is taking on the overflow, resulting in forgetfulness.

James had difficulty emotionally connecting with his wife and children, so he isolated himself in his garage—even sleeping there. He felt so guilty for not feeling emotion and sharing love with his family that he was determined to end his life over it. James truly felt that his family was better off without him (the post-deployment version of himself).

Getting Better

It's important to do an emotional spring-cleaning to ensure that our minds aren't clogged with unresolved and unprocessed toxic thoughts and emotions. Deciding to make a change is the first step, but knowing which course of treatment to follow can be overwhelming. Here are some approaches depending on the outcomes you're seeking, the time you want to take, and the level of investment you're willing to make.

Psychotropic Medication

Many people want to experience emotional healing with the simplicity of taking a pill. Taking psychotropic medication means that you recognize and acknowledge that something "just isn't right" in your life and now you're ready to make a comfortable change. Perhaps after you feel stable on your medication, you can add psychotherapy. Research proves that the most effective treatment for symptoms of posttraumatic stress is a combination of psychotherapy and medication. But if the thought of reliving the most terrifying experiences of your life through psychotherapy (talk therapy) is just too much right now, that's okay.

If you're considering taking psychotropic medication, think of it this way: You really want to have a beautiful front yard with plush green grass, but you don't have time to pull weeds. Instead, you simply mow them down to the same height as the grass; it blends, and you're good to go. But that only lasts until the weeds surpass the height of the grass. Your symptoms of posttraumatic stress are like those weeds and hiding them is like taking psychotropic medication. They keep growing at a rapid rate, but you can take medication that helps you feel "normal" and allows you to blend in. That's good for the temporary moment, but not long term. Pulling the weeds out by the roots, so that their return is slim to none, is like undergoing intensive psychotherapy on the topic of your trauma. Pulling out the weeds by the roots will take more time and dedication than mowing them down, but the results are long-term.

I would recommend that James undergo intensive exposure therapy with the help of psychotropic medication to manage his hypervigilance. Eventually, James will be able to wean off the medication, as he will have processed his traumatic events and recalibrated his sympathetic nervous system (alert system). Psychotropic medications can be viewed like training wheels that are removed in time once the trauma has been digested. And any type of treatment with Jesus at the center will be the catalyst to successful healing.

Exposure Therapy

Exposure therapy is just what it sounds like: being exposed to something unpleasant during therapy. It sounds daunting, I know. But as a psychologist, I don't make my veterans jump off the high dive at their first session. I may ask you to simply step into the water. Then I'll teach you how to dive—over and over again. Then you'll begin diving off the lowest-level diving board. Before you know it, you'll be jumping off the high dive. This may take place over the course of ten lessons. Initially, your fear of diving might have been ten out of ten. After completing your training, your level of fear will be zero out of ten.

Behind the closed doors of a therapy room, we're not capable of transporting you back to your deployment to reenact all the terrifying events that occurred. However, we are capable of having you relive the experiences in your mind. The first time you tell your story, it will feel awful. But you'll feel proud of yourself and a huge emotional weight will lift from your body. Dr. Dave Grossman brilliantly wrote, "Pain shared is pain divided."[†] These words could not be truer.

James will have to emotionally relive the traumatic events that occurred on his deployments in order to become desensitized to the images over time. He will also have to work with his therapist on becoming unstuck from his twisted guilt and self-blame for the lives lost on the battlefield, as well as his perception of himself as a monster. This process will eventually bring him peace of mind.

Distraction: Staying Busy

Our brains are wired to find solutions. You love a high operational tempo because it distracts you from your traumatic past. You will notice that as your tempo begins to slow, your anxieties increase. This is often observed as we approach the end of our military service. As they say,

---

[†]   Dave Grossman and Loren W. Christensen, *On Combat: The Psychology and Physiology of Deadly Conflict in War and Peace* (Millstadt, IL: Warrior Science, 2008).

an idle mind is the Devil's playground. When we're bored, our minds can gravitate to the unresolved or incomplete tasks we have mentally assigned ourselves but have not yet completed, uncomfortably resting on the aspects of our lives that feel unresolved. If your operational tempo has slowed, take advantage of this time to seek treatment for your overall well-being. Your psychological health strongly influences your physical health and the health of your most important relationships.

The slow pace of his block leave caused James to feel as though he were going crazy. He felt that he would have been better off back in Afghanistan, as his level of hypervigilance was conducive in a deployed setting. James much preferred keeping himself busy in the motor pool to sitting idle in his home, where he was triggered and haunted by past memories.

Accountability

Now that you know why all this is happening, you are accountable to get help. You can no longer claim "Ignorance is bliss." For the sake of your loved ones, please reach out. If you won't do it for yourself, do it for them. Be aware of your actions and how they may be impacting those around you. You aren't the only one feeling this way and experiencing these things. Please, put your pride aside and get the assistance you need and deserve.

Relapse

Relapse happens. What is relapse? It's when you fall back into old and unhealthy ways of thinking and acting while in the midst of treatment or after it. Sometimes, our brains fall back to those old and unhealthy neural networks versus the new ones we worked so hard to create: The good news is that relapse is part of recovery. When it happens, acknowledge it, shake yourself off, and move forward, continuing to implement all the good you've learned. It may be best to let your support team know so they may encourage you and show compassion.

Faith

Do not for one second believe that God is indifferent to your hurt and pain. More than anyone else, Jesus Christ endured horrific emotional and physical suffering. The trauma of being crucified on the cross for speaking the truth and spreading love, hope, and healing is unimaginable. History tells us that Jesus Christ was brutally scourged with a whip multiple times across His entire body. His wrists and ankles were nailed between bones to a cross. Jesus Christ shed His blood for hours on that cross before His final suffocated breath. As if that weren't enough, a crown of thorns pierced His head. The selfless sacrifice of Jesus Christ allowed us the glory of eternal salvation in His love.

> Fear not, for I am with you; be not dismayed, for I
> am your God. I will strengthen you, Yes, I will help
> you, I will uphold you with My righteous right hand.
> (Isa. 41:10 NKJV)

I strongly believe that Jesus wants us to confront our hurtful past experiences and make peace with them, and here's why: one of the most traumatic events of all time was witnessing the death of Jesus. Several of His loved ones, mother and disciple included, watched Jesus take His final breath. Many more witnessed His brutal beatings and public humiliation. These images undoubtedly caused PTSD in the observers who loved Jesus. When Jesus returned upon His resurrection to show that He had defeated death, He also chose to heal the minds of those He loved from the trauma they witnessed and bring them peace and closure. His return, through His resurrection, ensured they had to confront their past experiences with Him, good or bad, and make peace. If Peter, the disciple who denied Jesus three times, did not make peace with Jesus and his own past, do you think he would've had the courage to push forth the gospel with such passion?

Avoiding the painful aspects of our lives may work temporarily but certainly won't work long-term. The longer we avoid painful experiences, the more emotionally detached and distraught we become. Let's confront our past and make peace with it once and for all. This new-found peace will have a positive ripple effect on all areas of your life. Your loved ones will be the first to notice and appreciate the courage you mustered to confront the demons of your past. Let's explore the common themes that keep us stuck in the chaos of our minds.

Chapter 2

CONTROL IS AN ILLUSION

EQUATION: Reality in Training
$$A + B + C = D$$

EQUATION: Reality in the Fog of War
$$A/v + x + Bz + y + C + mx + B = WTF?$$

*Let's ask ourselves again: Are we
really in complete control?*

TSgt Paco's Story (USAF)

Technical Sergeant (TSgt) Paco was a large Puerto Rican man from New York City. He made it known to everyone that it was his privilege to serve the deployed troops—something he took great pride in. His message to his kitchen squad: "You never know if one of our meals will be their last. That's why every meal has to be perfect!" He enjoyed controlling every detail and would do anything and everything to bring a smile to your face when you walked into *his* dining facility (DFAC). He was the master chef, the food server, the waiter, the host, and the entertainment—everything—bringing life to a place that felt so dead!

Every green-suiter wanted to be on the same deployment with TSgt Paco because, with him as head cook, the taste of the food instantly transported you from a war zone to your comfort zone—the taste of home. His cooking was like magic and worthy of savoring. And for many, his meal *was* their last.

Working under TSgt Paco was inspiring and exhausting. He demanded perfection. A pastry chef before entering the Air Force, he enlisted because he wanted to give back. He swore that he would only serve one term, but then he fell in love with the "bigger purpose" of his job. Naturally, he could've made more money running his own independent business, but that wasn't nearly as fulfilling for him.

When TSgt Paco was ordered to take time off, he entrusted his DFAC operations to Senior Airman (SrA) Kim. She was nearly as OCD as he was and so fast that everyone referred to her as the Energizer Bunny. She could cook, chop, bake, wash, prepare, present, and open shop faster and better than everyone but the Sarge himself. He invested his time and energy to groom her to continue his demanding legacy, as he was quietly contemplating separating from the USAF after eleven years to return to his wife and young daughter.

He enlisted because he wanted to give back.

SrA Kim was barely five feet tall; her height nearly disqualified her from joining the military. She was a Dreamer from South Korea who grew up in NYC—like TSgt Paco—and she was working to obtain her citizenship for herself and her family. Her father was a hardworking man but lost his job because of cultural discrimination. Consequently, she took it upon herself to become the family's sole breadwinner. She took care of everyone in her life, especially her kid brother who had a diagnosis of Down syndrome. Every breath she took was in service to someone else.

SrA Kim didn't quite have the charisma of TSgt Paco, but she was endearing in her own ways. She spoke too quickly and buzzed like a bee throughout the DFAC. The more stressed she became, the redder her face and the more pronounced her Korean accent. If you somehow made her mad, she would curse like a sailor in Korean (at least, it looked and sounded like that). Her fits were a source of comic relief, and she knew it. At one point, SrA Kim was the most impersonated Service Member on the FOB (forward operating base), and she relished the spotlight.

On December 12, 2009, two mortars hit the DFAC at lunch. The C-RAM (Counter-Rocket, Artillery, Mortar system) that typically warned and shot down "incoming" was non-operational that day. Seven lives were lost and dozens of others were injured. The left side of the DFAC was destroyed. Smoke, fire, and rubble created a hazy gray blanket that obstructed aid to the victims.

TSgt Paco survived but sustained extreme shrapnel wounds to his arms, back, and legs with lacerations that penetrated layers of his flesh. Despite his injuries and the unrelenting ringing in his ears, he rendered care to all those who were wounded. He tied tourniquets and assisted in performing combat life support. He had kept extra medical kits around the entire perimeter of the DFAC as an added precaution, and every single one of them was used that day.

Once he finished securing victims and transferring their care to the medics, TSgt Paco continued searching for more casualties and found SrA Kim lying in a pool of blood behind the food dispensary. She had been decorating pastries when the mortars hit. One of her legs lay neatly beside her, as if she had placed it there herself. The other was hanging on by strands of flesh.

SrA Kim was holding her cross necklace and praying in a soft whisper. She reached out to take TSgt Paco's hand. "It's too late," she whispered and slowly shook her head with the little energy she could spare. "Make sure to let my family know that I love them, and give them the money."

Her words sounded Korean, but intuitively he knew exactly what she was saying. "No. You're not going anywhere," he responded. He wrapped her legs in tourniquets.

"Thank you," she said as she coughed and blood spilled from the corners of her mouth.

TSgt Paco tenderly scooped her up in his arms and shouted for the medics. They ran toward him carrying an empty litter saturated in someone else's blood. As he placed her on it, her breath slowed, her eyes closed, and her pulse disappeared. He pulled her from the litter and placed her on the floor where he attempted to resuscitate her for nearly thirty minutes; no one could pull him from her. SrA Kim died with a soft smile on her face and the indentation of her cross necklace pressed into the palm of her hand.

TSgt Paco lost his mind in that moment. He flipped tables and kicked chairs while screaming nonsensical profanities into the air. He didn't stop until his eyes fell upon her pastries. Half the pastries had icing zigzags; the others were unfinished. But nothing was more disturbing than the droplets of blood sprayed across them. Ironically, these were her favorite mango-filled pastries. He couldn't understand how one second, she was icing these pastries, and then the next, she was blown into pieces on the floor.

TSgt Paco didn't take any time to mourn. Instead, he kept so busy that he could barely think of anything other than reopening the DFAC and feeding his troops. *He was adamant about not letting the enemy win his emotional battle; they would not keep him down, nor would they stop him from rebuilding his passion from the ground up.*

After being sanitized and fortified with T-walls, the DFAC reopened with shifted mealtimes to throw off the enemy. Before the mortar attack, two eight-by-ten-inch pictures—one of TSgt Paco and the other of SrA Kim—hung at the entrance of the DFAC. The pictures were recovered, surprisingly not burned, and the old frames were replaced. Whoever rehung SrA Kim's picture didn't know that she had died.

The night prior to their reopening, TSgt Paco took cover in the DFAC from a sandstorm outside. His goal was to set up all the equipment for his squad prior to their arrival at zero dark thirty. He stopped in his tracks, feet planted firmly like magnets to the ground as he stood in front of SrA Kim's picture. For one moment, he closed his eyes and pretended that she was still there, a busy bee in the kitchen executing his orders.

Just then, the winds pushed through the DFAC's front door, knocking SrA Kim's picture from the wall. He caught it with both his hands just before it hit the ground. He pulled the picture close to his chest and slid down with his back to the wall until he sat hunched on the floor. Finally, he allowed healing tears to flow.

Prior to deployment, SrA Kim designated TSgt Paco as her sole beneficiary. She was concerned that the payout for her life insurance would not make it to her family because they were not American citizens. No one expected her death—no one.

As a final act after deployment, before returning to his own loved ones, TSgt Paco met with the Kim family. He spoke about their daughter with great pride and admiration and gave them her life insurance funds. He made a strong and enduring connection with Kim's younger brother. As with all things, TSgt Paco went above and beyond.

TSgt Paco strongly believed that he was supposed to be in control of all things DFAC related. He felt responsible and blamed himself for much of what happened that day ... for the lives that were lost ... for SrA Kim's death ... for the building's infrastructure not withstanding the blast ... for not finding and accounting for SrA Kim fast enough ... for the lunch hours he'd selected ... for the incoming alarm not sounding. And he also blamed God.

Training and Battle Space

The military has good intentions when it teaches you to believe you're in control of your battle space. You rehearse battle drills with vigor. In fact, you don't just learn to do something in the military—you're pushed beyond that. "See one, do one, teach one." Just replace one with one hundred.

You're rightfully taught that if you let your guard down for one moment, it could cost the lives of you or your battle buddies. The military teaches you to believe that you and your squad are in *control* of your battle space at all times. Such a belief instills confidence in you. The more confident you are, the better you will perform. If you lack confidence, you succumb to uncertainty, which is costly in war. Uncertainty can result in lost time and poor choices that produce fatal outcomes.

However, the illusion that you're in control of your battle space comes at a cost. If a tragic event happens, you blame yourself because you believed you were in control. The more you buy into the idea that you have full control, the more responsibility you place upon yourself when bad things happen. When responsibility is taken to the extreme, particularly when events are not within our control, severe psychological damage can result. It's important to find the balance and appreciate room for improvement when reflecting on an after action review (AAR).

When good things happen, we tend to experience self-satisfaction and joy. But it's temporary and short lived. We often share the responsibility of a good thing with others—and bask in the glory together. But when bad things happen, we selfishly own it, we don't share it, and we hold on to it for a lifetime, allowing it to manifest into shame and twisted guilt. This is the voice of the Enemy; listening to it is your consent to your own imprisonment.

The Fog of War

Every aspect of war is based on the perception of it from different angles, none of which communicate to one another in full. Knowing and understanding the complete context of war from everyone's perspective is impossible because there are so many variables that cannot be controlled or accounted for. In other words, no party has the full picture of the battle plans. Critical decisions are always executed with incomplete intelligence. Remember, intelligence is never complete because there is always more information that we could learn and acquire about our enemy that we don't have full access to. You do not have control of these unknown and unpredictable variables. As a Service Member, you react to them to the best of your ability—and that's all you can do.

The fog of war is everything that alters your ability to see clearly in the midst of combat. It can be broken down into both macro and micro levels.

At the macro level, the fog of war concerns the ability to obtain as much intelligence about the enemy's mission and plan of execution as possible. Because of the nature of war and the objective to win, no single party invested in the fight knows every element of the big picture.

War compromises our bodies and minds. At the micro level, the fog of war negatively impacts the environment, bodily functions, and mental status, altering the decisions we make with regard to our tactical responses. We rely on our bodies and minds for our perception of reality. Think about it: exhaustion, pain, dehydration, hunger, fear, injury, grief, and the effects of climate—the list goes on and on. When your body is compromised, is your lens of the world more or less accurate? *Less.* In combat, we have to make decisions under all these extreme measures. This is why we practice repetitive battle drills with the goal of being able to function on autopilot when our environment overstimulates us.

Because of TSgt Paco's fog of war, on the macro level, he was not informed that the enemy would mortar the DFAC. Moreover, the alarm system was inoperable at that time. On the micro level, the fog of war compromised everyone's ability to render aid in an environment filled with fire, smoke, rubble, and debris. TSgt Paco had to provide care to others despite his own blast injuries. This is where his combat life support training kicked in, and all those hours of rehearsal were automatically executed at the right time and the right place. TSgt Paco had to think as clearly as possible to save lives, despite his compromised physical and mental faculties.

Understanding Influence vs. Control

It is more accurate to discuss the influence we have over situations versus the control we have over them. No one has full control of the events that occur in our lives. Control connotes that 100 percent cause and effect is due to our decisions—to act or not to act. Our own influence upon external stimuli is measured on a spectrum of low to high. The goal of the military is to achieve maximum influence over the assigned mission by the equipment we use, the intel we possess, the personnel we've trained, and their ability to perform while in contact with the enemy. However, since we can never predict all the variables at play on the battlefield, we will never have complete control.

For example, a sandstorm could occur in the middle of a firefight and significantly impact the outcome. The sandstorm is something you cannot control. But you and your squad have vehicles and weapons equipped to withstand the sandstorm, and you've trained under these conditions, improving your squad's level of influence over the circumstances—an advantage. Level of influence determines our advantage or disadvantage.

Do We Have Any Control?

For someone who has trained relentlessly and worked to stay alive, this may be a difficult message to hear. The good news is we have 100 percent control over our own reactions and perceptions to the world around us—that is, our thoughts, emotions, and behaviors. Our thoughts and emotions dictate our behavior. Only you can decide how you want to respond to the world. You can choose to listen to the Enemy and blame yourself for something you truly did not have control over, or you can choose to believe that you did your best in light of the circumstances and free yourself from incredible emotional pain.

TSgt Paco was adamant about not letting the enemy win his emotional battle—they would not keep him down—nor would they stop him from rebuilding his passion from the ground up.

Influence or Control over External vs. Internal Events

It's clear: we have *full control* of our internal functioning and *influence* over our external surroundings. Naturally, our internal functioning includes our thoughts, emotions, and behaviors—our responses and perspectives. External functioning includes how the world spins around us, the enemy's reaction, weather conditions, and everything addressed in the fog of war.

Sometimes it's difficult for us to grasp that we have no control over the external events in our lives—only influence over them. Perhaps that's why some of us believe the illusion that we have control (when we don't), as this idea somehow makes us feel safer and more secure.

Which statement would allow TSgt Paco to have emotional freedom from his guilt for the tragedy that occurred after the mortars hit the DFAC?

> A. "I was in charge of the DFAC. That means I had control of everything that happens within that scope. I failed to control the bad events that transpired when the mortars hit that day. I was in charge, so I take personal responsibility for all those who died in that event."

> B. "I did not have any control over how or why the mortars hit that day. Obviously, if it were up to me, that would've never happened—ever. I did my best under the tragic circumstances. I ignored my wounds to render combat life support to those who were more severely injured than me. I controlled my own fear reaction and turned that energy into life support skills. I had intelligently placed life support equipment throughout the DFAC—in more places than I needed—and all of it was used. I believe that I helped save lives in more ways than one."

The obvious answer is B. TSgt Paco had strong influence on saving lives after the mortar attack. However, he did not have any influence over where, when, why, and how the mortars landed. TSgt Paco took 100 percent control of his emotional response to that event. He did not succumb to his fears but rather he saved multiple lives in the fog of war. In the next chapter, we will address TSgt Paco's intentions and the death of SrA Kim.

We have no control over the external events in our lives— only influence over them.

Every enemy (Taliban, insurgents, ISIS, Satan, etc.) wants you to blame yourself for the tragic events that were not in your control, because as soon as you blame yourself, you wreck yourself. When you're emotionally wrecked, the Enemy (Satan) wins the psychological and spiritual warfare. The Enemy is a liar—so stop listening. Instead, tune in to the truth and remember what gave you the courage to be willing to lay your life on the line for your country.

Chapter 3

INTENTIONS ON THE BATTLEFIELD

What was *your* intention for joining the Armed Forces?

> To support my family
> To fight for my country
> To travel the world.
> To become a United States citizen
> To be a bada**
> To serve those who serve

I joined the Air Force to serve my country and to help heal those who fight for our freedom. Think back to your original intentions for joining the military. How we live our lives will be shaped by our intentions, which flow from our moral and/or spiritual compass.

Remember what you signed, Enlistment/Reenlistment/Commission Contract (DD Form 4/1):

> Required upon order to serve in ***combat*** or other ***hazardous situations***.

I remember thinking to myself, *I could die doing this*, when I signed my contract. As a psychologist, I wasn't going to be the tip of the spear and charge headfirst into combat, but I would be required to deploy to support the troops and their behavioral health concerns. Even if I wasn't part of the fighting force, I could still be in a war zone, increasing my odds of falling victim to the enemy that has a target on every American's head. I swallowed hard and I signed, determined that fear would not dictate my life or obstruct the path of God's calling for my future.

I imagine you signed with a similar feeling of gravity. I believe that if your military specialty was more operational (the tip of the spear), then you understood the consequences. As you signed the contract, you recognized that this might be the most profound and weighty document you would ever sign. You didn't go into this blindly; you were aware that you could sacrifice your life in the call of duty. Whether it was a reality we chose to recognize or dismiss, we were tracking the potential consequences. Yet we signed the most life-changing document we could potentially encounter. Understand this: even those who died while in the service understood what they were signing; as a volunteer force, we all do. It all goes back to free will and our choices (to be discussed in chapter 5).

The Crystal Ball

Imagine you have a crystal ball to predict the future. Even in ancient times of war, warriors sought soothsayers, oracles, and fortune-tellers to provide guidance on the battlefield. They hoped such tools would provide intelligence about the enemy and show the consequences of decisions before they transpired. Imagine if you could plow through combat without any losses and prevent the death of every Service Member.

Having a crystal ball isn't possible, but when you vigorously blame yourself for combat losses and assume responsibility for the actions of others, you act as if you had a way to predict the future. Remember, you were operating in the fog of war and there's no clarity under such circumstances. If you had a crystal ball to predict the future that day, would you have done things differently? Yes. You would've done everything in your power to prevent the loss of your beloved brother- or sister-in-arms. The very fact that you would have done things differently demonstrates the purity of your intention.

Your intention goes all the way back to the first question in this chapter. Naturally, your intention can evolve with time, experience, and the building of lasting relationships. Your original intention for joining the military may have been to make a better future for yourself through the educational benefits and training offered. But as the years passed, your intention may have evolved into a desire to stop the spread of evil that you witnessed on your first deployment. Now that you're an NCO or officer in a leadership role, with more than one deployment under your belt, your intention may have shifted to bringing every one of your Soldiers home to his or her loved ones. Just as we evolve as human beings, so do our intentions as Soldiers.

Twisted Guilt vs. True Guilt

Twisted guilt is when you blame yourself for an external event over which you had no control. You take on this responsibility because you felt you could've or should've done more or known better to prevent the injury or death of your brother- or sister-in-arms.

Twisted guilt is faulty because it occurs when you falsely convince yourself that you had *control of external events*; you're manipulating truth and reality. The key words here are *control* of *external* events.

In the last chapter we learned that we *never* have control of external events, only *influence* over them. This sort of guilt makes us prone to self-punishment as a means to reconcile our perceived wrongs.

Actual guilt occurs when your *chosen* behavior directly and negatively impacts another. For example, imagine a person receiving a letter explaining he owes $20,000 to the IRS. When he walks into his house, he's so angry at the IRS that he kicks his happy dog. After the emotional dust settles, this person feels guilty for being aggressive toward his dog. This is true guilt because the person had full control of his emotional response (internal stimuli) and chose to let negative emotions erupt and hurt an innocent bystander: the dog. This person could have chosen to behave differently.

Remind yourself: you did what you could in the fog of war and you didn't have a crystal ball to predict the future. Your intention was to bring everyone home to his or her family. You did your best with the limited knowledge you had at that time; don't pretend you had a crystal ball. You cannot hold your past self accountable for what you know now. That's absurd!

Ask yourself, *Am I using the concept of "hindsight is 20/20" to support my twisted guilt?* "Hindsight is 20/20" reinterprets the past with perfect vision because we've learned the outcome of our decisions. It's not fair to judge your past decisions with your present knowledge. It makes no sense for you to punish yourself for what you didn't know then, whether it was something that could only be acquired through experience, time, and development or whether it was the unpredictable variables caused by the external world.

For example, should an expert medic continually punish herself for losing a life on the battlefield, when at the time she was a novice whose only practice before that was on animals and in role-play? No. Though the hurt is valid, it shouldn't be enduring! It's possible that even with all the experience and resources in the world, that life couldn't have been saved. I'm certain the medic never intended to lose a life on the battlefield. Although bad outcomes may cause us to become indignant, they can be a catalyst to change so we may evolve for the better—sharpening our skills and enhancing our potential far beyond what we imagined for ourselves.

It's not fair to judge your past decisions with your present knowledge.

Think about any guilt you're dealing with. Consider how twisted guilt manifests inside you, causing you to feel angry and irritable, so that your loved ones take notice. Do you allow your mood to dictate your thoughts and behaviors with your family? If you act snappy, yell or raise your voice, or brood alone in your room, these are all legitimate reasons to feel *true* guilt. But the crazy thing is, you're allowing *twisted* guilt to make you feel this way!

The Enemy Loves Twisted Guilt

There are two battlefields in war: the one where your boots hit the ground and the one where you fight for your spirit (heart and mind). Which battlefield will you allow an enemy to win? *Neither!* Which battlefield do you have full control over? By the grace of God, the spiritual battlefield. It is here that you make many decisions to entertain either good or bad. What you choose to cultivate and nourish (good or bad) will inevitably thrive.

The Enemy, or Satan, loves your twisted guilt because it destroys your family, it destroys your connection to God, and ultimately it destroys you! The Enemy plants a toxic seed in your mind, and you choose to water that seed by allowing yourself to experience shame, self-isolation, substance abuse, anger, twisted guilt, thoughts of unworthiness—the list goes on. It slowly eats you from the inside out as you push everyone out of your life until you're alone in the darkness of your own despair. Could this potentially be worse than dying on the physical battlefield?

Don't allow the Enemy to win this battle; fight it for the sake of those who love you and, of course, for yourself. Here are four courses of action you can take:

Be ready. God knows that twisted guilt is a favorite weapon of the Enemy so He warns us, "Be alert and of sober mind. Your enemy the devil prowls around like a roaring lion looking for someone to devour" (1 Pet. 5:8).

Don't be afraid. The Lord knows what's in your heart and all your intentions. God knows the difference between true guilt and twisted guilt. "By this we shall know that we are of the truth and reassure our heart before him; for whenever our heart condemns us, God is greater than our heart, and he knows everything" (1 John 3:19–20 ESV).

Release it. God wants us to make peace with our past to make room for a new beginning. The past can easily be forgiven if you allow it. "Forget the former things; do not dwell on the past. See, I am doing a new thing! Now it springs up; do you not perceive it? I am making a way in the wilderness and streams in the wasteland" (Isa. 43:18–19).

Understand. Don't pay mind to the lies of the Enemy. Focus on God's truth and it will set you free. "We demolish arguments and every pretension that sets itself up against the knowledge of God, and we take captive every thought to make it obedient to Christ" (2 Cor. 10:5).

Replacing Guilt with Self-Compassion

If one of your brothers- or sisters-in-arms approached you about his or her guilt and suffering related to loss on the battlefield, I'm certain you would show that person love and compassion—but why do you refuse to give such compassion to yourself? Self-compassion is not a weakness; it is a strength.

Before you can truly love and accept others, learn to love and accept yourself. "There is no fear in love. But perfect love drives out fear, because fear has to do with punishment. The one who fears is not made perfect in love" (1 John 4:18).

The toxic seed of guilt grows like a weed, and it thrives when we give it our time and energy. Often, we nourish it with alcohol, anger, detachment, and isolation. On the flip side, if you stop watering and nourishing your guilt, *it will stop growing and eventually die.*

Instead, have you considered planting a seed of life? Plant it—even if the toxic seed is still thriving. The two will compete. If you nourish the seed of healing, it will grow more powerful and more quickly than the seed of toxicity. The two cannot coexist for long. As you begin to pour more energy into your healing, you may find yourself logically processing to the source of your twisted guilt. You'll identify what needs to change in order to improve your quality of life. You'll begin to see your thoughts and experiences differently—through a healthier and more adaptive lens. This is when you'll decide to stop the Enemy from winning the psychological and spiritual warfare.

What do you do when you logically know you aren't guilty but you *feel* guilty? Don't worry—that's completely normal. Be patient. Sometimes our thoughts and emotions are incongruent with each other, which tends to elicit anxiety. Give your emotions time to catch up to your new, healthier thinking patterns. These fresh thoughts you've planted need time to take root and grow. After all, you've allowed the Enemy's toxic seed to thrive for too long!

The toxic seed of guilt grows like a weed, and it thrives when we give it our time and energy.

Once you decide to leave twisted guilt behind and transition into self-compassion, how will you occupy your time? It's imperative to find new and healthy activities to promote positivity and healing and distract you with a sense of purpose as your soul heals. Even if it feels forced at the beginning, reconnect to your favorite hobbies and interests; they will help bring you peace and satisfaction. Whether it's spending more mindful time with your children, becoming your son's or daughter's Scout leader or soccer coach, volunteering for a meaningful purpose (Habitat for Humanity, Big Brothers Big Sisters), attending church small groups, or beginning a new hands-on project (woodworking, cars, art), jump in and give it your all.

Only you can determine what feels right for you and how long you'll need to complete your healing. As humans, we tend to feel the most love and validation when we practice acts of serving and giving. Ultimately, we must fill the void of our hurt with love—the love of God.

Peace and Revelation

After three months of weekly treatment for his PTSD, TSgt Paco began to see his circumstances more clearly. He discovered that twisted guilt dictated his life and his interactions with the world. He began to harbor feelings of true guilt for how his twisted guilt damaged his relationship with his wife and daughter. Once he came to this realization, he made peace with SrA Kim's death. Here TSgt Paco discusses his intentions:

> **Interviewer:** If you had a crystal ball to predict the future, would you have done things differently?

> **TSgt Paco:** Of course! I would've evacuated the DFAC and made sure that everyone was accounted for and safe. But I had no control over these events— we were all caught off guard.

> **Interviewer:** What was your intention for SrA Kim after she got hit?

> **TSgt Paco:** Naturally, to save her life. If I had somehow known that she was hit, I would've searched for her immediately. I did what I was trained to do. I medically triaged the individuals I had direct access

to in order to maximize my time and efficiency, and time under these circumstances means life or death. I helped to save more than one life that day. I did my best to save SrA Kim and I believe she knew that.

Interviewer: What was your intention for your relationship with SrA Kim?

TSgt Paco: To groom her to be a great cook. To open doors for her future and her family's future. I was invested in her, almost like a father would be invested in his daughter. She was going to continue my legacy.

Interviewer: Why did you join the Air Force?

TSgt Paco: As you know, I could make so much more money if I owned my own bakery or restaurant. But I had a spiritual calling to join and to help those who fight for our freedoms. I wanted to give them a piece of home when they were off fighting. I know it sounds cheesy but it's true—ask my wife. She doesn't like the fact that I'm so damn passionate because it separates us. I need to put my family first now.

Interviewer: When you reflect on all your intentions, what do you notice?

TSgt Paco: I'm pretty damn proud of myself. I followed through with every goal I had in the military. I know I wasn't one of the bada** SF guys, but I sure as hell was the best chef they ever had. I also know in my heart that SrA Kim is at peace. She is filled with the love of God. I understand now that God does not will bad things. I am, however, grateful that the Lord placed SrA Kim and her family in my life. When I think of her now, I don't see her last moments. Instead, I see the first time she tried a mango pastry. That smile and the flaky buttered crust spread across her lips. I will see her again.

TSgt Paco returned to the East Coast and opened a new bakery with SrA Kim's family. This partnership was a divine connection, and the bakery became the most popular in town. In remembrance of her loving spirit, every year on SrA Kim's birthday, the bakery sends thousands of mango pastries to the overseas DFACs to spread love to the deployed service men and women.

"For whenever our heart condemns us, God is greater than our heart, and he knows everything" (1 John 3:20 ESV).

Reject the lies of the Enemy around control and guilt that only bring destruction. Instead, know your truth in light of God's Word—it will set you free. In the next chapters, we will come to learn about God's journey with us through our hurt and pain. We will learn about how much God loves us and has never forsaken us. Remember, Jesus (fully God and fully man) was not immune to the pain of this world. Neither are we.

Chapter 4

DEATH IN COMBAT

Peace in the Eye of the Storm

"If They Could Speak"

You're still holding on to me—and that's okay. But I don't appreciate how you choose to hold on to me. You're tethered to me with so much hurt and suffering. You're tethered to me with anger, hate, and guilt. You're tethered to me with should'ves, could'ves, and would'ves. All you see of me is the image of my last moment in life—my worst moment—breathless and physically broken.

I am the kite tethered to you by a line. The line that connects us is a toxic energy of emotional hurt. I'd prefer you let me go—as such a connection pains us both. But you won't let me go. Because if you let me go, you believe my sacrifice will have been in vain—forgotten. So I understand that you need that tether. But I ask you to replace the toxic line. Please cut our connection of pain and suffering. I don't want that energy connected to my spirit, nor do I want to be the source of your hurt. If I sacrificed my life so you can have yours—live it well, live it free, and live it loved. What's the point in having sacrificed my life if you're beating yourself up, pushing your loved ones away, and contemplating suicide? You're letting the Enemy win the spiritual warfare, and that disappoints me, my friend.

You must beat the Enemy that has infiltrated your heart and mind. Start by tethering me to a line of love and gratitude so that you and I may have peace. Replace your last memory of me with the time I made you laugh so hard you pissed your pants. Live your life now in the ways I couldn't live mine. I'm content and at peace here; there's no need to worry about me. I assure you that my existence is much sweeter than yours. I'll see you in time, my friend....

God is merciful to us in the way He has designed us, especially in our suffering. Even in the transition from life to death, God is with us, bringing the peace that passes understanding. For those comrades you lost in combat, believe with your whole heart that God was with them through the journey of transition. Do not let the Enemy convince you that the one you lost was abandoned and left for dead. If you were with that person for his or her last breath, God undoubtedly used you as an extension of His love.

What follows are some descriptions from *survivors* who have experienced the transition from life to death. The common theme of these spiritual experiences is peace and an overwhelming sense of God's love.

Andrew's Encounter (US Marine)

On this deployment, it wasn't a matter of if I was going to die, but rather a matter of when. I had been waiting for death for a while now. Every time I laced up my boots, I paused to make right with God. And the fact that it was finally here felt like a relief.

I couldn't feel anything. My heart pounded in my ears. The warmth emanating from my legs and through my body was comforting. I attempted to understand the sensation by lifting my body to take a look, but the medic threw my torso back to the ground. "You're gonna be fine. I got you." He pinned me down and stared into my eyes. Somehow his soul reached deep and down into mine, as if to revive me. In that split second, I wanted to reverse the process of my dying because my brothers needed me—and I needed them. But that didn't matter to the force that pulled me from my body.

I hovered over myself. The medic forcefully clapped his hands around my cheeks, again and again, calling me to return, "Rivera. RIVERA. RIVERA!" The sound of my name reverberated through me, but the direction of the sound transitioned from down below to up above. My focus began to widen—wrapping me in a panoramic view of everything. One of my legs was missing. Another leg was placed behind the medic, and one arm was obliterated. Jesse and Caleb were dead—their bodies were unidentifiable—the medic didn't know who they were—but I knew. The answers kept flooding my mind—questions and words were not necessary. And with one breath, I was back in my body for one pulse, until I ascended into what appeared to be a tunnel or vortex with a bright light at the end. The sh** was real. My consciousness rocketed through the tunnel and toward the light of comfort and healing. Like magnets drawn together, I needed to be in that light. Words cannot describe what it was like once its magnificence surrounded me. At the other end of the light were brilliant colors—colors I had never seen before. The answers continued to flow into me—I finally understood. Jesse and Caleb were here, but as soon as I ventured to find them, my heart guided me away from their experience to focus on my own. I can't believe I'm saying this, but I was completely immersed in love. I was safe and at peace. As soon as my mama approached me, she kissed my cheek and whispered, *"Te amos, mi hijo."* And then I fell backward through the vortex. The sound of the falling became the humming of the air evac's engine. My spirit fell into my body, and I took my first breath of awareness. That's when the pain spread through me like a wildfire.

Many Service Members who have been shot or blown up and lived to share their emotional experiences express eerily similar encounters. Peace, comfort, safety, warmth, and love are consistent themes in the stories of those who have transcended the flesh to embrace the spirit after undergoing horrific bodily trauma. Pain is not something they describe in the immediate moments or even hours after the ordeal. Naturally, the farther the spirit departs from its vessel (the body), the more the consciousness becomes in tune with the connection of love and peace. However, the closer the spirit is to the body, the more connected the consciousness is to the chaos of reality.

Take comfort that if you had to watch a friend transition from life to death, his or her experience was most likely much like the account above. Remember, fear and confusion may initially dominate, but when that settles, peace and love override. Our God is a merciful God.

Many Service Members have had near-death experiences (NDEs) that have changed their lives forever. The International Association for Near-Death Studies has made itself available to provide free support services to veterans who have undergone an NDE and are trying to make sense of their lives in light of that event. Most believe that an NDE is a miracle.

If you were with that person for his or her last breath, God undoubtedly used you as an extension of His love.

Our Perception of Pain

God is so merciful to our flesh. After experiencing terrible trauma to our bodies, He doesn't allow us to be consumed by pain and suffering. Instead, certain neurotransmitters—like norepinephrine and serotonin—block the pain signals. When trauma impacts the body, our sympathetic nervous system goes into fight-or-flight mode, and "superman chemicals," like adrenaline, take effect. This neurochemical excitation blocks the pain signals from registering and can last for more than an hour. Believe it or not, in the heat of the moment, a paper cut in an office may be perceived as more painful than having a limb blown off in combat.

Let's say you are in a small room with your favorite guitarist—perhaps Carlos Santana. Imagine your pain detector is like an amp. You can hear the intricacies and nuances of Carlos's fingers hitting the strings through a small amp; it's so precise and clear. This is like the pain of a nasty paper cut in garrison. You can feel the slice and separating of the skin as the air hits it. In contrast, imagine that the entire

Metallica band has joined you and Carlos in that small room, and every single musician is connected to that solitary amp. Do you think you can hear any one musician clearly? Absolutely not. The crazy distorted amplification of the signal (by the sympathetic nervous system) results in the "washout" of the original signal. This is like the washout of the perception of pain due to the flooding of adrenaline and all sorts of neurotransmitters throughout the spinal cord.

The Final Moment: On Repeat

The final moment of your battle buddy's passing was just that—a moment. I'm certain your brain has burned that awful image into your memory. Why? Because memories tied to strong emotions, such as fear and sadness, are remembered more vividly. It's a survival mechanism.

Don't allow that tragedy to

continue to live on—for the

sake of your peace and his.

The tragic, final moment with your comrade is, sadly, how you've come to remember him. In the grand scheme of his incredible life and his valiant battles, this is what you take with you. Would you want someone to remember you as a mangled physical body in its last moment? No. This vivid image of pain and suffering causes you to relive both your torment and his. It keeps your comrade frozen in the worst moment of his life, forever. You become so stuck on that image, it's hard for your brain to logically believe the moment has passed and that it was just *one* moment.

Don't allow that tragedy to continue to live on—for the sake of your peace and his. I know you refuse to forget your buddy, but consider replacing the image of his death with one of the craziest, stupidest, most hilarious, or most soul-connected moments you ever had together. Revisit that awesome image in your mind, over and over again, until it replaces his darkest moment. Rewiring the brain takes time and repetition. Make the investment; it's worth it.

The Enemy Didn't Beat Me

The first time I read the book of Job in the Bible, I got it all wrong. But I thank God for a Soldier who clarified the book for me as he related Job's story to his own struggles.

One day, Satan approached God about His loyal follower, Job. Satan informed God that Job only glorified Him because the Lord brought prosperity to all aspects of his life. Satan taunted the Lord and said that Job would curse God's name if he were to lose all the wealth God had afforded him. God insisted that Job would remain faithful under all circumstances. The Devil vowed that this was not the case and asked to test God's belief. To prove Satan wrong, because good never bows down to evil, God gave Satan control of all that Job possessed. But God commanded Satan to spare Job's life.

Satan destroyed everything that belonged to Job, from his wealth to his family. Job did not cave to Satan's wish for him to curse God. Instead, Job continued to surrender to the Lord with more love and conviction until all was restored.

In the book of Job, God did not cower before the Devil and allow him to prove his slanderous theory true. Nor did Job cower before the Devil's destruction. Instead, Job turned his head to God in continual surrender. We do not allow evil to thrive even if it may result in death and destruction. As you know, there are two battlefields: the one where boots hit the ground and the other of the spirit. The Enemy shall certainly not win that of the spirit.

From Death Notification to Present

A Non-Commissioned Officer (NCO):

I hated that job, I really did. I know hate is a strong word, but that's how I felt about it. Watching the government vehicle pull up, seeing us step out in our Class A uniforms, hats in hand—the families knew. Some refused to open the door—delaying the inevitable. They all knew they had lost their loved one. I can't tell you how hard it was to steel myself for them.

I won't ever forget the woman who beat me up. Being that I'm a large man, it was not an issue. I let her, of course. If being a punching bag for her was the only way I could support her grief, I'd be that, and I was that. But it hurt emotionally to see her crumble the way she did upon learning of her husband's death. Just before the Chaplain and I left, about an hour later, she collected herself, apologized, and hugged us both. I made it a point to remember that moment, because in one hour, she began to heal right before our eyes. It was a rapid transformation as the Chaplain spoke the Word of God to comfort her soul. I knew that one year later, she'd be doing better with time, family, our support, and of course, God on her side.

I was right. I Facebook-stalked her because I needed my closure too. Her page was filled with pictures of her with her children and grandchildren. Her smile was real; you could see it in her eyes. She posted a prank video that her kid grandson had made at her expense.

I couldn't care less about the prank itself, but what I listened to—over and over—was her laughter. I know she's never been the same since that day, but I also know that she found love and happiness once more. In true stalker fashion, I scrolled her Facebook feed to the anniversary of her husband's death. There was a picture of their wedding day posted with the comment, "I look forward to the day I will look upon you again in the kingdom of God."

"If They Could Speak" (continued)

Just because I died at the hands of the enemy doesn't mean the enemy beat me. Never. You see, when evil spreads, we have an obligation to battle it. Evil is not allowed to thrive and infiltrate a land of defenseless people until it robs us of our homes on our soil. Beyond the grave, I continue to stand against evil. My death represents my willingness to fight until the end. It is something I am proud of. Someone will always have to die in battle, on both sides. It is a sacrifice for the waging of war. I stood firm on the side of our Lord during battle. I am humbled to be a lamb, as He was mine.

Even though I walk through the valley of the shadow of death, I will fear no evil, for you are with me; your rod and your staff, they comfort me. (Ps. 23:4 ESV)

We often hear this verse at services for those we have lost as a reminder that God is with us and will never leave us. He wants us to feel the peace and comfort of His presence. God loves you so much that He gave His Son for you. "For God so loved the world that he gave his one and only Son, that whoever believes in him shall not perish but have eternal life" (John 3:16).

This is God's absolute love. Let's look at this a little closer, as I suspect you may have some questions about where God was when you walked through the valley of the shadow of death.

Chapter 5

WHERE IS GOD IN WAR?

Greater love has no one
than this: to lay down
one's life for one's friends.
—John 15:13

As a warrior, you know the immeasurable value of a life sacrificed. Yet the greatest sacrifice for the sake of love came long ago and will continue long after we're gone. Every story in this book revolves around the truth that true healing can only be found in perfect love, and perfect love is found at the expense of one life: Jesus Christ. "Then you will know the truth, and the truth will set you free" (John 8:32). Free from what? Free from the lies of the Enemy that have held us captive to spiritual and psychological destruction for too long.

If you only take one thing away from this book, let it be this: *If it's not love, it's not God.* But who is God?

God is life. God is not the author of the hurt and suffering in your life or in the world around you. "The thief comes only to steal and kill and destroy; I have come that they may have life, and have it to the full" (John 10:10).

God is love. "God is love. Whoever lives in love lives in God, and God in them" (1 John 4:16).

Faith has been known to be the most powerful source of a person's resilience. This chapter serves to answer the questions "Why do we suffer?" and "Where is God during our suffering?"

What Is Our Purpose?

God created humankind to love and be loved! Believe it or not, we're neurobiologically wired for this. Only humans were made in God's image (see Gen. 1:27) for the purpose of relationship. In order to have relationship, God gave us free will—the power to choose. Our freedom to choose and make decisions is a substantial gift God gave to us because of His love for us. We are the only species on the planet with the ability to override our survival instinct. Think about it—no other animal ever chooses to end its life by suicide.

If God took away our free will because our choices are often wicked, would we still be capable of having a relationship with Him? No. Taking away our free will would make us like robots, programmed to do whatever God wants. Our Father is interested in relationship and not ownership; He doesn't control us by overriding our free will. God loves us even if we choose to defy Him and deny Him. God's love for us is perfectly selfless and holy (set apart).

The good news is that even in our rebellion and the resulting shame that separated us from God, He loved us so much that He sent His Son to take on our sin and restore our relationship to Him (see John 3:16–21).

Where Does Evil Come From?

If a holy God and His selfless love are at one end of the spectrum, who and what are at the opposite end? Satan and his selfish desires. Evil is the absence of love and the absence of love is sin.

Selfishness leads to other evil, as it is the catalyst for murder, theft, war, rape, greed, and the list goes on. When our brains detect a threat to the "self," fear may cause us to do bad things in order to protect ourselves.

The big picture: war begins when a person or a group of people places their selfish wants, needs, and beliefs above the freedoms and benefits of others. It can also be triggered by fear, a natural response to threat. "For where you have envy and selfish ambition, there you find disorder and every evil practice" (James 3:16). God is not responsible for our wickedness; we are!

"God is light; in him there is no darkness at all" (1 John 1:5).

Where Did Evil Begin?

It all began in the garden of Eden—paradise. God intended for humans to always live in His immediate and loving presence. "And the LORD God commanded the man, 'You are free to eat from any tree in the garden; but you must not eat from the tree of the knowledge of good and evil, for when you eat from it you will certainly die [spiritual death]'" (Gen. 2:16–17).

God instructed Adam and Eve not to eat the forbidden fruit from the Tree of Knowledge of Good and Evil. God informed them that they would lose the personal and intimate relationship they shared with Him, as good cannot coexist with evil (much like oil and water don't mix).

Why Did Adam and Eve Eat the Forbidden Fruit?

Satan tempted Adam and Eve with their own selfishness—the idea that they could become "like God" (Gen. 3:5). Essentially, they chose to place their wants and needs above the commands of their Creator. As the first people, Adam and Eve made the ultimate decision for all humankind, and sin infiltrated the world because of their choices. Since that moment, the Enemy has continued to deceive us into choosing selfishness—the source of our demise—and destruction.

How Do You Think God Felt?

As a loving God, He never wants us to experience pain and suffering. However, if God had stopped Adam and Eve from their decision, they would not have possessed free will, the precursor to a loving relationship with Him.

Every day you have choices to make that will determine your life consequences. You can choose to eat from the Tree of Life, which produces all good things in line with God: love, truth, wisdom, freedom, and joy. Or you can choose to eat from the Tree of Knowledge of Good and Evil, which produces all bad things in opposition to God: selfishness, bondage, and inevitably, death. If you plant good seed, then surely good fruit will grow (see Gal. 6:8). If you choose to sow bad seed, then you will reap bad things. If you choose to place Jesus at the center of every aspect of your life, you will reap what Jesus sowed: a life of abundance that God has declared for you. The choice is yours.

Does God Care about My Suffering?

No one is immune to suffering—not even Jesus! In order for God to have a relationship with us, He had to first relate to us, so He sent His holy Son Jesus. Because He was both fully God and fully man, Jesus understands what it's like to be human and He empathizes deeply with the experiences of humanity. Even in His perfection, Jesus allowed Himself to be tempted in every way, just to remind us that He, too, has been here—but most importantly, He has overcome! He was then put to death in the most horrific way. If Jesus, the Son of God, was not immune to the hurt and pain of this world, what makes us think we are?

Jesus gladly chose to sacrifice His life so we may have eternal salvation and walk again in God's loving grace, as Adam and Eve enjoyed before the fall.

Is God Punishing Me?

God is the one and only perfect dad. His love is perfect, and if we trust in Him and wait upon Him, His answer to us is always "yes" and "amen" (2 Cor. 1:20). He does not teach us or punish us by bringing any form of evil into our lives. In fact, He will blow our minds with His incredible grace. Grace is the unearned, undeserved, and unmerited favor that God grants us despite our fallible nature. God wants us to run to Him when we find ourselves in trouble—whether we or someone else caused that trouble. Would you want to run to a punishing God who desires to teach you by using hurt and suffering as lessons? No way! Our God is a God of love and trust. Would you place your own child's hand on a hot stove to teach her not to touch it? Of course not! Similarly, your Father handles you with great love and care. Remember, if it's not love, it's not God.

Does God Forgive Me?

No one is free from sin. God wants nothing more than for us to seek His forgiveness when we recognize our wrongdoings. "If we confess our sins, he is faithful and just and will forgive us our sins and purify us from all unrighteousness" (1 John 1:9). When we demonstrate awareness and accountability for our actions going forward, we demonstrate our love for God. We will falter more than once, and that too is forgiven. "I tell you that in the same way there will be more rejoicing in heaven over one sinner who repents than over ninety-nine righteous persons who do not need to repent" (Luke 15:7).

How Good Is Good Enough to Get to Heaven?

Have you ever worried that you might fall short of entering heaven because the good deeds of your life do not add up to enough? News flash: your good deeds will never be good enough. Instead, it's the sacrifice of Jesus that is enough. It's simple: forgiven people go to heaven. As established in the Old Testament, forgiveness requires sacrifice, and that sacrifice is Jesus. All you have to do is believe that Jesus died on the cross for your sins, that He was broken so you could be made whole. With a genuine heart, simply ask for forgiveness, and your loving Father will grant it to you.

Does God Like War?

Of course not. God operates on the frequency of love and peace. But I believe God understands that war may be necessary, especially when fighting to protect our freedom, home, and country. It is also our responsibility to stop evil from impacting innocent lives. God is not a pushover; hence, God does not expect us to be pushovers. "For I, the LORD, love justice; I hate robbery and wrongdoing. In my faithfulness I will reward my people and make an everlasting covenant with them" (Isa. 61:8).

Does Everything Happen for a Reason?

Let's be clear: God is good, and He desires good. When events happen in our lives, whether good or bad, we can create our own reasoning for them. With the help of God, we may choose to convert the consequences of the bad events into something positive and productive.

"And we know that in all things God works for the good of those who love him, who have been called according to his purpose" (Rom. 8:28).

These are just the basic questions about God and His role in life and war that I've encountered in session with my combat vets. You may have many more questions now, but I'm hoping this is creating a comfort level for you with me and the potential role that therapy can play in your healing. Now, I'd like to invite you inside the therapy room to show you how sessions work and, hopefully, convince you that your life can change for the better.

Part II

In Session with Combat Veterans

*Witnessing the healing that takes place
behind the closed doors of therapy*

Therapy is key to healing, but fear of the unknown can prevent us from receiving the help we truly need. I'd like to invite you into a few sessions so you can see what goes on behind closed doors and be encouraged by the life-changing work that is accomplished. Let's begin by explaining the process I have developed to bring healing to individuals who have experienced spiritual and psychological trauma from their combat experiences.

What Is Rhythm Restoration (RR)?

Rhythm Restoration is a means of healing that I've refined throughout the years and will demonstrate in the next several chapters. It's a scientific protocol that uses faith as a catalyst to healing. Yes, I just wrote the words *faith* and *science* in the same sentence. If God created everything, then He created science; it's that simple. I've come to believe that science is a tangible way to appreciate God's miraculous creation. Science is mesmerizing and can strike a sense of awe and wonder, further strengthening our faith in God. RR is used to help bring spiritual and psychological peace to our past experiences through reflection, as well as create positive future interactions through visualization. Below is a step-by-step breakdown of how RR works.

The Four-Part Answer
1. Confronting the Hurt to Move On

The Bible tells us to move on from our hurtful past and instead look to the new things God has in store for us. Isaiah 43:18–19 states: "Forget the former things; do not dwell on the past. See, I am doing a new thing! Now it springs up; do you not perceive it? I am making a way in the wilderness and streams in the wasteland." In order to move forward the way God instructs, we must make peace with our hurt and find closure in our suffering. We must invite God into our painful experience so He may bring us the peace that "transcends all understanding" (Phil. 4:7). The hallmark symptom of posttraumatic stress is avoidance. Avoiding our psychological hurt delays our emotional peacemaking (which could bring relief) and worsens our symptom presentation. The more we confront something that scares us or pains us, the less scary and painful it becomes.

2. Rhythm

As you grew in your mother's womb, the beat of her heart accompanied your development. Rhythm comforts the mind and body, and regulates us emotionally and physically. When we're anxious, we tend to tap our hands or feet, bounce our knees, or even rock back and forth to soothe ourselves. It has been proven that rhythm helps regulate our autonomic nervous system, having a calming effect on our minds and bodies. *"Walk with me and work with me—watch how I do it. Learn the unforced rhythms of grace. I won't lay anything heavy or ill-fitting on you. Keep company with me and you'll learn to live freely and lightly"* (Matt. 11:29 MSG).

3. Bilateral Stimulation

Have you ever noticed how your brain goes a million miles an hour when you're on a stroll, jog, or run? Most of us come up with our best ideas during that time. This movement has an ingrained rhythm to it, in addition to a right and left movement (bilateral stimulation). Engaging in bilateral stimulation triggers both the right and left hemispheres of the brain, activating the brain's processing system. In the same way that the stomach digests food, the brain has to digest thoughts, emotions, and experiences. Bilateral stimulation serves as an effective catalyst in filing away important memories associated with learning, from academics to assembling a weapon.

Bilateral stimulation occurs during rapid eye movement (REM) sleep when your closed eyes move back and forth. However, when we're asleep, we're unconscious. Can you imagine how powerful bilateral stimulation would be if we were consciously aware of what we were choosing to process? Although our minds prefer to avoid hurtful experiences, if we choose to confront those hurtful events for the purpose of emotionally digesting them (to end the pain), a combination of bilateral stimulation and rhythm helps reduce the psychological indigestion. Research tells us that bilateral stimulation helps us to reintegrate our painful or scary experiences, stored in the fear center of the brain (amygdala), into our regular, nontriggering, not-scary, long-term memory (semantic memory). To engage bilateral stimulation in session with my participants, they tap their hands on their legs, alternating right and left, while using their own unique rhythm.

4. Imagination and Visualization

Believe it or not, the brain has a difficult time deciphering the difference between real and imagined experiences. Imagined experiences lay down effective neural networks and, when repeated in our minds, they gain strength over time. Think about it, our SF (Special Forces) guys, and even Olympic athletes, visualize perfecting their physical objective to improve their actual performance. Albert Einstein once said, "Imagination is everything! It is the preview of life's coming attractions." Everything we possess today has come from someone's imagination. The Bible says, "For as he thinks in his heart, so is he" (Prov. 23:7 NKJV). If you imagine yourself successful and moving toward healing, so it will be. If you imagine yourself despairing and spiraling toward destruction, so that will be.

Within our minds, we can re-script hurtful experiences and replace past pain with hope and understanding, aiding in our psychological digestion. I'm not suggesting that we lie to ourselves, but the best part of our imagination is that it is capable of creating a new and healthy neural network in our brain, replacing the old and painful network of your traumatic experience. I'm asking us to see God in every aspect of our lives because He never abandons us.

Even the Bible encourages us to use our imaginations. Ephesians 3:20 states, "God can do anything, you know—far more than you could ever imagine or guess or request in your wildest dreams!" (MSG). You know what that tells me? To dream *big* and imagine *wildly*! But if that's not enough, imagine this: "Therefore I tell you, whatever you ask for in prayer, believe that you have received it, and it will be yours" (Mark 11:24 ESV).

What Does RR Look Like When We Put It All Together?

It's simply closing your eyes to assist in visualizing a particular prompt as directed by your mentor, all while alternating the tapping of your hands on your lap at your own unique rhythm. Rhythm Restoration is about disconnecting from our thoughts and perceptions so we can allow the Holy Spirit to reveal what we've missed and restore us to who we were meant to be. It's about receiving the wisdom and knowledge of God, and in doing so, we take back control of our thoughts. This shifts our perspective from what was once wrong or hurtful in our lives to where God was, is, and will be in His promise for our future. Essentially, with Christ at the center of our healing:

> We must CONFRONT the emotional hurt
> with a combination of RHYTHM for soothing,
> BILATERAL STIMULATION for psychological
>   digesting,
> and positive VISUALIZATION for the re-scripting
>   of painful experiences.

> We destroy arguments and every lofty opinion raised against the knowledge of God, and take every thought captive to obey Christ. (2 Cor. 10:5 ESV)

> Can you imagine the breathtaking recovery life makes, absolute life, in those who grasp with both

hands this wildly extravagant life-gift, this grand set-
ting-everything-right, that the one man Jesus Christ
provides? (Rom 5:17 MSG)

To signal its use during a session, this method will be noted as *<Rhythm Restoration>*.

Chapter 6

KILLER OF INNOCENCE

Zuma is a fictional character whose emotional experiences accurately reflect those of many combat veterans.

Name:	Zuma Gonzalez
Gender:	Male
Age:	41
Ethnicity:	Mexican American
Branch / Rank:	Army / SFC
Time in Service:	19 years
Military Occupation:	11 B; Infantry
Deployments:	6; Iraq and Afghanistan

A black hole of emptiness and loss overwhelmed my ten-by-twelve-foot office that day—a force of hate, anger, fear, guilt, and insurmountable sadness so strong it was as if the clouds blocked the sun. A beast of a man, the size of a linebacker, sat hunched over, head in hands and elbows on knees—an upright fetal position—the posture of catharsis. Toxic thoughts and emotions escaped him, running free in a glistening stream of tears and mucous, settling on the old blue carpet. Free from shame, the great dam finally crumbled, allowing tides of emotion to rip through every dry place in his soul. This event needed to be witnessed and accepted by someone who could be an extension of God's love and grace. Let's back up …

Session 1

When I brought Zuma back to my office from the waiting room, I felt like the *Fearless Girl* statue set before the massive *Charging Bull* statue in New York City—except this bull had succumbed to the girl. With each dreaded step he dragged his feet, keeping a cold distance of five feet behind me. I stopped twice to wait for him, and at each pause he avoided my gaze. He sat with a thud in the middle of my sofa and it responded in discomfort. He had *that* look on his face: *Who the f*** are you?* and *How could you possibly understand?*

After spending a moment on logistics and protocols, I asked for permission to share a little about myself so he would see me as a real person and not a walking textbook—not just as an impersonal, snooty psychotherapist.

I maintained eye contact, fearing he would emotionally slip away to a place deeper than where he was a moment before. Where he'd slip away to was what I had yet to discover.

He raised his perfectly shaped eyebrows and gazed past me to the wall decorated with diplomas and other accolades. His eyes quickly and diligently scanned the room as if he were on a patrol.

"You were military?" he asked, only raising one of his perfectly tweezed brows.

"I was." I smiled gently and silently reached for the picture on my desk, then held it out for him to see, allowing him to ascertain the time, place, and situation.

"I'll be damned! Good to see you rolled in the mud too!" He clapped his hands like Thor. In the picture, my battle uniform is covered in mud and sand and I'm standing on a beach after rucking with Special Forces.

Zuma threw himself back against the couch, and the cushions protested. "Well, okay then," he said as he continued to observe the contents of my office. He ran his fingertips over the military coins awarded to me over the years. With his curiosity satisfied, his gaze returned to mine and he asked, "How do we do this?"

She's gonna leave me if
I don't get help.

"Let's start with what brings you here."

He planted both feet firmly on the floor. "My wife. She's gonna leave me if I don't get help." He ran his fingers through his crew cut. "I don't blame her," he said, and then sighed and shrugged his shoulders.

Good, he has accountability, I thought. It dawned on me that his wife was responsible for sculpting his perfectly tweezed eyebrows. Indeed, she must have a powerful influence over this man's life. Zuma had accountability to a strong woman and motivation to change—a winning combination.

"What would your wife say about you if she were here?" I asked. Military spouses are so incredibly strong. They, too, endure the battle.

"I'm not the same. After each deployment it got worse." He shifted in his seat trying to get comfortable. "I've been on six," he said, covering his eyes with both hands. They slid down his face, over his lips, until finally they fell into his lap, palms up, still and defeated.

Once a devout Catholic, Zuma had lost his faith in God, believing he had broken "too many" of the Ten Commandments to go to heaven. He went through the motions of attending Mass to placate his wife. He explained how emotionally detached he felt from her and their children, and from the world at large. Each time the spiritual community applauded his combat valor, he pulled even further away from God and the church. He imagined God maniacally laughing at him because He knew the truth. This Soldier insisted that God inflicted his psychological torment as punishment—with no end in sight.

Zuma and his wife had two sons, ages twelve and seven. He loved them dearly but didn't know how to show it. Instead, he yelled and withdrew from his family—he hated himself for that. Zuma felt helpless and trapped to repeat the same wrongs, again and again.

He spoke about how impossible it was for him to connect with his youngest son, Ezra. He couldn't understand why he avoided him the most—terrified of bonding with him in the way he had bonded with his eldest. Something was blocking his love and preventing it from reaching his youngest son.

He mentioned a birthday party where he had lost his cool with Ezra. He explained how the littlest things now irritated him to an unimaginable degree. Ezra had neglected to pick up candy wrappers left behind from the piñata smashing. Zuma pulled him aside and gave him a tongue-lashing, so much so that Ezra asked to leave the party. Once home, Zuma realized, *What child asks to leave his best friend's birthday party?* At that point, his world came crashing down.

With the fortitude of a stubborn bull, Zuma plowed through his anxiety in crowds, sleep deprivation, flashbacks, and nightmares filled with pink mist, screams, and detached body parts. But he couldn't continue to live without his love reaching Ezra.

☆ ☆ ☆

Session 3

Among those sitting calm and collected in the waiting room, Zuma sat with his legs bouncing out of control. He had a white-knuckled grip on the handles of the chair to prevent him from flying out of his seat.

It was nothing shy of a miracle that Zuma kept this appointment; it was a testament to his motivation to reach his son Ezra. He had nothing to lose and everything to gain. The weight he carried would begin to lighten; bit by bit it would slowly be eliminated, like peeling an onion layer by layer and tear after tear.

Zuma was ready for battle and engaged his "combat breathing" as he followed me to my office. (Our Soldiers prefer that term to the traditional "deep breathing.") He psyched himself up to tell me about the one atrocity he swore he would never bring back to life. He wanted it dead and buried, but the only way he could actually kill it would be to confront it head-on. Zuma had no option but to bring peace to the roaring riptides; today we would figure out how.

My couch was dreading his visit, but I was ready. As I shut the door behind us, I whispered under my breath, "God, help me, help us." Side by side, we took our places on the battlefield. It was time.

"You look worried," I said as I rolled my office chair nearer to him.

He sighed heavily, almost a rumble in his breath—never once did his eyes meet mine.

"It seems like you've been stressing about today. You're here. That's half the battle," I said, waiting for a response. Together we sat in silence for several of his pounding heartbeats.

Zuma finally looked at me, his eyes glossy and almost hollow. He saw me catch my breath in response to his gaze and quickly averted his eyes back to the floor. Somehow, I saw too much, straight into his soul. Suddenly, he popped up and began pacing the room like a caged animal.

"God, help us," I whispered under my breath again.

He stopped and sat heavily back into his seat. Then, like water from a fire hose, the words gushed from him; the fire had to be put out—now!

"That day in Iraq, I volunteered to go out on a mission in place of my buddy." He shook his head. "It was supposed to be my day off, but he was having an online argument with his wife about some dumb Facebook post she made. His mind wasn't where it needed to be. He needed to get his sh** straight to be good for the next day's mission." Zuma released a hot breath of air from his nostrils. "I basically forced the guy to stay back. Man, I should've just let him go, but that doesn't matter anymore. At least I spared him from the horror of that day."

He paused, took a deep breath, and looked at the roll of tissue I'd strategically placed near his seat before he arrived. He unrolled about eight sheets and slowly tore at the perforated lines. "Just in case," he said, holding my gaze for the first time this session.

I nodded reassuringly.

Zuma's brows furrowed. They were more unkempt than usual (problems with his wife, I figured). He spoke slowly and thoughtfully. "That day's mission was different and unexpected, but it was supposed to be good. I needed to go on it; I needed to see something other than death." His right fist pounded the sofa to make a point. "This mission was meant to win 'the hearts and minds.'" Zuma made air quotations with his fingers. Then he reached for the water bottle near his foot and took a swig to keep the tears at bay.

After clearing his throat, he swung the bottle in a circular motion and then set it down. He returned to staring at the floor. "We loaded the trucks with food, water, candy, stuffed animals, and balls. All kinds of balls: footballs, soccer balls, even cheap-a** colorful plastic balls. I remember one ball was red, white, and blue with stars. It caught my eye. We tested the toys for the kids—actually, more like we broke them in." He laughed softly and then paused. Zuma took a long, drawn-in breath, preparing to plunge deep into the dark waters without oxygen.

"It was a beautiful day—hot as hell—but as beautiful as that sh**hole would ever get." He shifted on the sofa. "Once we got to the village, the kids came running out to our trucks. We parked a safe distance from the homes; we didn't want to intrude on their space." His hands squeezed the life out of the edge of the sofa. "Kids"—Zuma shook his head—"they weren't afraid of us. Just motivated by the candy and colorful balls—the sh** our kids think is lame." He pushed out a muted half laugh. "There were almost two dozen kids there, all between the ages of three and ten. You know, they're small for their age—malnourished, I guess." He looked up at me matter-of-factly, and I nodded.

He continued, "We spent an hour tossing balls and riding bikes with lollipop sticks hanging from our mouths." He allowed a small but genuine smile to break through his stone-cold expression. "The village never heard so much laughter and so many high-pitched squeals of joy. I'm certain of that." Zuma took one quick breath in and out of his nose, and then he steeled himself to press on.

"This one kid—he reminded me of my son. They were both about the same age, four or so. I gave him the biggest and shiniest plastic ball—you know, that patriotic one I mentioned. He loved the sh** out of it. We rolled and kicked it back and forth. He must've fallen over a dozen times—each time picking himself up, laughing." Zuma's eyes filled with tears. "I can't remember exactly how he looked, but I do remember how his eyes lit up with excitement—almost like a cartoon." He looked at me and his laugh turned into a sob. "He was so damn happy. I'm grateful I could give that to him." His voice cracked. "F***! Why did it have to be like that?" he asked as his knees bounced out of control.

He clenched his teeth and then forcefully formed the next few words. "The children were"—he hesitated—"called to return back to the village by some man speaking Arabic. Whatever he said, it didn't seem to alert our interpreter, so we carried on, picking up candy wrappers and chewed lollipop sticks. It was a good day until …" Zuma sat shaking his head and wiping his sweaty palms on the sofa. A continuous stream of tears poured down his cheeks.

"That little boy … the one I gave the patriotic ball to, peered from around the corner of one of their shacks. He was about fifteen meters out." Zuma used the toilet paper to pat the beads of sweat forming at his hairline. He wiped his entire face in one circular motion, but it didn't do any good because the tears didn't stop. "Still happy as sh**, the boy bounced toward us holding what appeared to be flowers. They were bright and colorful—obviously fake." Zuma blotted his clumpy wet eyelashes to see more clearly. His voice quivered when he said, "For one millisecond I thought maybe it was a thank-you gift." He pushed out a guttural half laugh. "How f***ing stupid was I? This kid was getting closer to us, and then it registered. Some f***er put a suicide vest around his chest and tried to hide it behind the fake flowers he was holding." Zuma's fists pounded the edge of the sofa. "I shouted at the platoon, *'Everyone take cover! He's wired! He's f***ing wired!'*"

Zuma covered his face with his hands, and his entire body convulsed. He remained quiet—the seconds filled with our pounding hearts and his tears.

He spoke more quietly than before. "The interpreter shouted at the kid in Arabic and told him to stop, but he didn't." A whimper escaped from Zuma's throat. "I swear it, that boy was looking at me. He was running toward me—still smiling—ready to give me those flowers. He was completely clueless."

He held his head in his hands as he bawled, and then he looked straight at me. "Doc, there was no mistaking that the vest strapped around him was a bomb."

"Yes, Zuma. I believe you," I said, our shared pain confirming he wasn't alone. I gestured for him to continue, and his breath wavered, in and out.

"*'Shoot him!'* our commander shouted. My dumb a** was closest to the gunner's turret, so I mounted. *'F***ing shoot him now! Dammit! Or we'll all die,'* he screamed at me." Zuma's breathing hastened, and his body went into fight-or-flight mode.

"When I looked through the scope, the boy seemed unaffected by the chaos he was causing. All I could think about were my children and how I needed to get home to them. No one was going to take that away from me—not that day." Zuma stomped the floor.

"I pulled the f***ing trigger, and he exploded. He f***ing vanished into pink mist." Zuma looked me straight in the eyes. "I'm a child killer—a killer of innocence." Zuma fell sideways on my couch and sobbed. I didn't stop him; he needed release.

"I'm still here," I whispered after watching several minutes of his catharsis.

"But I wish I weren't," he responded, and then he pulled himself upright.

"Why?" I dared to ask the question I knew the answer to, but I needed him to articulate it himself, aloud.

"Because I took the life of a child," he said in an irritated tone.

"You did because you had to. That day, you saved your entire platoon. You sacrificed your moral integrity to save their lives," I said in a stern voice.

"How come you see it like that? How can you even stand to be in front of me right now?" Zuma reached for the toilet paper and kept unrolling it.

"I believe you're a good man, Zuma. That day you were forced to choose between the lesser of two evils and then act on your decision and a command, no less." I stared deep into his eyes. "I can see you this way because I'm not you. I'm an objective observer; you're not."

He seemed shocked at my response—almost like he didn't want to believe he was good because he was so used to believing he was bad.

I pulled my notepad and pen from my desk, and I asked, "What was your intention for the mission that day, Zuma?"

"To bring joy to the children. I wanted my team to feel good for once—like we made a positive difference. We needed to experience something other than destruction." His face turned hard and he grunted. "Dammit!" He shook his head and then immediately resumed his combat breathing to help maintain his bearing.

"Your intention was beautiful, Zuma." I leaned toward him and asked, "If you had a crystal ball to see into the future, would you have done something different that day?"

He tilted his head and looked up. "Absolutely. The little boy would still be alive. The kids would've gotten their toys in a hasty drop-off—no one gets hurt—too easy." He paused to process his thoughts. "Why did God let that happen if we were doing something good? And why did He make me the killer?" He threw his hands up in frustration.

"Zuma, God doesn't will bad things to happen to His children. God gave us the gifts of free will and creation; that's how we were created in His image. No other creature has free will."

"Right." He straightened up and sat attentively, resting both hands on his knees. "Survival instinct is what drives animals; they can't override it the way we can," he said.

Pleased by his participation and insight, I fed off his energy. "Exactly. Sometimes we make horrible choices that cause others and ourselves great suffering. What is the root of all evil?" I asked as I crossed my arms and stared pensively at him.

"Damn. That's a loaded question. I don't know. How about war? Or murder?" He shrugged.

"Fair enough. Why would someone choose to commit murder or war?" I asked.

"Power and control. When someone places their wants above someone else's well-being, I suppose." He leaned in, resting his chin on his hand.

"Right. How about selfishness?" I could tell he was listening. "Would you say that selfishness is the precursor to war or murder?"

"Yeah, definitely. That makes complete sense." He nodded and then wiped the snot from his nose.

"Humans are inherently selfish creatures. Evil arises from our selfishness," I said, switching my crossed legs and putting down my notepad.

"So I was selfish when I shot the boy?" he asked in an angry tone as his expression tensed.

"You were protecting yourself and others—but let's wait to grasp the big picture before we jump to conclusions."

"Roger," he mumbled.

Then I asked, "Tell me about the fall of man."

"Back to Sunday school, huh?" He laughed smugly. "Adam and Eve, right?" I nodded. "Well, they were the first humans. They lived in a perfect paradise with God. They were tight with Him. But they ate the apple that God told them not to. Then everything went to sh**!" In an animated fashion, he made a popping sound with his mouth, demonstrating an explosion with his hands.

I smiled and said, "You're right. God created us to live in paradise, forever. He never intended for us to experience anything other than love and goodness. God wanted a relationship with us, and that's why He gave us free will." I paused to let him process. "Can you have a relationship with a robot?" I asked.

His eyes widened, he threw his hands up, and he comically replied, "That's the only kind of relationship I *could* have right now." We both laughed—a much-needed tension breaker. He continued, "But realistically, no. A robot is like a slave. It has no choice. A relationship needs to be a decision made by those involved." He paused to think, and then asked, "If God wanted a relationship with us, why did He sabotage it by placing the tree in the garden of Eden in the first place?" He looked boggled with his hands on his head.

"Well, we needed a way to demonstrate our free will, right? God was fair and just when He told Adam and Eve the negative consequences of eating from the Tree of Knowledge of Good and Evil. Nevertheless, their curiosity got the best of them, and they went against God's request. It was a selfish decision. Eating the fruit was their choice, not God's."

He sat still and hunched. His eyes darted back and forth as he processed the information. Then an answer came to him, and he sat up tall and straight in his seat. Zuma said, "The serpent deceived Adam and Eve. He told them they'd be like God if they ate from the fruit that would bring them knowledge of evil." He pinched his chin between his index finger and thumb. "The serpent was evil and selfish in his deception. Selfishness is a theme here!"

"Exactly. All those Sundays in Bible study are paying off."

He quickly nodded. He took a long, drawn-in breath, and all of a sudden, the storm clouds parted in his head—another epiphany. "God didn't put the vest on that boy. It was that piece of sh** that did it." Zuma paused to absorb his revelation, but the storm clouds quickly returned. "But why didn't God stop him?" he asked angrily.

God didn't will any of this; everyone involved had a choice.

"Good question. Let's tackle it together," I said, making our search for answers a team effort. "If God controlled our actions, would we have free will?" I asked.

"Of course not!" Zuma stated. "And if we don't have free will, we can't have a relationship with God, the purpose of our creation," he continued. His neurons kept firing, making one connection after the next.

"All right. Let's put your experience into perspective. What have you learned about your situation in light of God's love?"

He nodded and took a deep breath before speaking. "I acted out of self-defense and for the protection of my battle buddies. God didn't will any of this; everyone involved had a choice, and each person's choice impacted the next person's choice."

I tried to stop myself from interrupting, but I couldn't help asking, "If you didn't shoot the boy, would he have survived?"

His mouth dropped. "No. I don't know why I didn't see it that way before. With the vest on, he was gonna die anyway. Shooting him before he got closer saved my entire platoon." He ran his fingers through his hair. "Oh my God."

I let Zuma sit with that big thought for a moment before asking, "Did God will this evil?"

"God would never will that. The man who strapped the child into the vest made that f***ed-up decision. I hate that man with all my being," he said.

"Better you hate him than God," I replied.

"Yes, you're right," he said with a lightness in his tone that I hadn't heard before.

"Zuma, what was your intention that day?" I asked.

"To love those children, despite our war."

"Do you think God can forgive you?" I asked.

Zuma stared at me and without hesitation said, "Yes. I do."

☆　☆　☆

It takes time for us to shift from old to new thinking patterns. Zuma spent many sessions discussing his concerns about his faith. He journaled about his life experiences and how they fit his new perspective of himself and the world. He read his new thoughts daily, sometimes multiple times a day. He put a tremendous amount of effort into his healing and the rewiring of his brain through Rhythm Restoration.

Every day we have the opportunity to choose between life and death. When we choose death, we consume the words of the Enemy and become prisoners deprived of hope. The Enemy tells us we are unworthy, doomed, unlovable, and other depressing lies. Yet, when we choose life and consume the words of God, we live free and fulfilled. God tells us that we are worthy, chosen, loved, forgiven, blessed, and the list goes on.

Zuma finally accepted that he was forgiven, and soon he'd come to recognize that he is loved and so much more.

Session 3 (continued) ...

"Zuma, I want you to drift back to the most painful experience during that deployment." As I encouraged him to skim through that deployment in his memory, like a movie in fast-forward, he began alternately tapping each knee as his mind sorted through the most hurtful events of that time.

<Rhythm Restoration>

After nearly a minute of tapping, I cast a lifeline into his darkness, hoping he would take hold of it. "Zuma, tell me what you experienced," I asked softly.

He looked up to focus on me. His eyes were glossy and his cheeks were wet. "My son. What I saw in my mind—he was the one wearing the suicide vest. It was my son's face. The boy and my son were the same age at that time." He deliberately pointed his finger, as if the visualization of his son was standing before him.

The planets in Zuma's universe began to align for the first time in too many years. Tears chased one another down his face as he looked out the window.

Self-discovery and the connections we can make with our subconscious promote the most effective healing. Though I had been aware of the relationship between the boy in the vest and his son, I held on to it until he came to recognize it himself. If Zuma hadn't made that connection, I would've led him to it before our time expired.

He covered his mouth with his fingertips and looked at me with wide eyes. "It makes sense. That's why I lost my sh** with the candy wrappers at the birthday party. The candy wrappers triggered my memory of the moments just before that event."

Thank You, God. I repeated those words in my mind.

He spoke softly, "I felt so guilty for taking someone's son that I imagined what that pain would feel like if someone took my son the same way. I punished myself by trying to experience that hurt," he said as he reached for more tissue to wipe his face.

"Yes, Zuma. Your brain twisted that tragic memory into your own self-punishment and stored it deep in your subconscious until now," I said.

He straightened up and wiped his sweaty palms on his ACU (Army Combat Uniform). "Doc, tell me what to do. How do I fix it? I don't want my son being a part of this equation."

"Let's rewire your brain with a new visualization. Can you remember the face of the young boy?" I asked.

He shook his head. "No, only the face of my son." One tear escaped and began rolling down his face until he aggressively wiped his cheek with his palm.

"All right. Let's visualize the boy's face as a blurred image." He nodded. "Now, bring the image of the boy in the vest to mind but with his face blurred."

<Rhythm Restoration>

While I waited for his mind to process the image, I prayed that the thoughts running through it would promote his healing. My heart raced and my breathing quickened.

"What did you experience?" I asked urgently.

"He's not my son. That young boy's face returned. I remember him now."

The tears that fell down Zuma's face were different from those that had fallen during our first few sessions. Today's tears contained healing properties, while the others were toxic, having formed from anger and twisted guilt.

Zuma said, "The young boy had a bushy unibrow, huge eyes, and his skin was ashy around his thin, dried lips. The kid was cute as hell." A low, rumbling laugh escaped from him. "I can see that boy as clear as day. He was so happy when he looked up at me." Zuma didn't bother to dry his face.

"How does it feel to see him instead of your son?" I asked as I continued to navigate the river of healing.

"A relief, but also a lot of sadness."

"I want you to rewrite that horrible day in your mind. Allow peace to preside over the outcome."

When he closed his eyes, his lips quivered and tears gathered at his chin as he fell into a peaceful and gentle rhythm.

<Rhythm Restoration>

"What did you experience?" I asked.

"The young boy came closer to me, still wearing the vest, but I wasn't scared. As he approached, he was surrounded by a glowing light." He blotted his face with a tissue. Zuma looked at me and whispered, "The vest just fell away." His breath fluttered when he inhaled. Then he laughed and said, "I know this sounds ridiculous, but a man came for the child and took him away." He cupped his eyes with his hands. "But then as the boy was leaving, he stopped and turned around to look back at me." Zuma's voiced cracked when he said, "He waved goodbye to me and then continued his journey. What did I do to deserve that?"

"Grace: the unearned, undeserved, unmerited favor of God," I whispered.

I fought back the tears but was unsuccessful, so I let them flow. I took in a congested breath and asked, "What did that visualization mean to you, Zuma?"

He didn't hesitate in his response. "The boy is at peace—free from the hurt experienced in his short life. Anyone who would strap this innocent child into a suicide vest didn't deserve him," he said with clenched fists.

"A few sessions back, you mentioned that the boy seemed oblivious to the circumstances going on around him. Do you take comfort in that?" I asked.

"Yes. He was looking at me, coming to me. He found comfort in me. I will always regret the circumstances, but at least he left this world innocent and filled with joy. His death was painless: here one minute, gone the next."

"How did you feel when you played soccer with him?"

"Connected. Loved. I imagined that I was playing with my son." Zuma's head dropped and he whispered, "Ezra."

I steeled myself against the back of my chair to help me maintain my composure. "I want you to visualize the young boy and the man with whom he walked into the distance."

<Rhythm Restoration>

"What did you experience?"

"Ma'am, it was Jesus who was with him. This time, I waved goodbye."

☆ ☆ ☆

Session 6

"Zuma, I want you to visualize yourself approaching Jesus, and I want you to ask Him how He sees you. Do you think you can do that?" I asked.

"Whoa. That's deep, but yeah," he replied.

<Rhythm Restoration>

"What did you experience?" I asked.

This man no longer harbored an ounce of shame for crying. He didn't even bother to wipe his tears before he spoke. "Jesus showed me His scars, and He reminded me that I wasn't alone in my suffering." His lips trembled, and he remained silent for several moments. "He called me 'warrior,'" Zuma continued. "He placed His hands on my shoulders. He was actually bigger than me." We both laughed. "But He told me I was strong and worthy of love—that He loved me. Jesus loves me!" he proclaimed in victory. "Then He said that the boy is looking forward to meeting me someday and playing ball again." A rogue tear slipped from the corner of his eye. "Jesus said to keep going and to fight for Him. I left the image wearing gold armor and carrying a sword. I'm ready—now more than ever."

"Therefore put on the full armor of God, so that when the day of evil comes, you may be able to stand your ground ..." (Eph. 6:13).

At our last session, I had the privilege of meeting Zuma's family. Ezra walked into my office swinging his father's hand back and forth, his eyes bright and filled with life. His wife and other son followed close behind. His wife had a peaceful look on her face. The first words out of her mouth were "Thank you. You brought him back to us." I smiled, shook my head, and pointed upward. She understood my gesture.

I reminded Zuma that God would do everything to find him, and He did; God found him in the darkest of places and pulled him back into the light. In that same way, Zuma was relentless in doing anything and everything he could to find his connection to his own son Ezra.

Chapter 7

FLATLINES

Lindy is a fictional character whose emotional experiences accurately reflect those of many of our combat veterans.

Name:	Lindy Porter
Gender:	Female
Age:	48
Ethnicity:	African American
Branch / Rank:	USAF / COL
Time in Service:	10 years
Military Occupation:	Medical Doctor
Deployments:	2; Iraq and Afghanistan

Session 1

"COL Porter?" My eyes searched the sea of olive-drab green in the waiting room, and a petite African American woman stood up and waved at me. Hanging tightly to her left arm was a sprite, perhaps five years old. "Who is this?" I asked as I crouched down, resting my hands on my knees. The little girl's rosy cheeks were kissed in freckles the color of butterscotch. Her frizzy blonde curls were gathered into poufy ponytails atop her head. But the icing on the cake was what she was wearing: a child-size version of her mother's ACU. She was a military doll come to life.

"Camilla." She sharply pronounced all three syllables of her name. "But you can call me Cammy." Before I could squeeze in a word, she continued, "I'm going to be a doctor too!"

"Yes, Ma'am! You will be." I saluted her and she saluted right back. The pair followed me down the long corridor to my office.

I'm trying so hard to lock up my emotions.

As I held open my office door, Cammy ran to the sofa, climbed up, and patted the seat beside her, urging her mother to sit with zero distance between them. COL Porter placed bulky, pink headphones over Cammy's ears, and the little girl proceeded to stare, transfixed by a young woman speaking with lively gestures on her pink iPad.

"What brings you in today, COL Porter?"

"Please call me Lindy." She flashed a contagious smile at me while surreptitiously pointing a pulsating index finger at her daughter. "She's why I'm here," Lindy whispered as she looked at Cammy from the corner of her eye.

"I see. I apologize for being distracted, but what's she watching on her iPad?" I asked.

Lindy's eyes began to well up. "No need to apologize." Tears streamed down her jaw. "She's watching …"

"It's okay." I rolled closer to her in my chair. "I don't want to push you out of your comfort zone too quickly."

She nodded her head and slowly pulled the collar of her beige undershirt up to smother her tears, careful not to draw Cammy's attention to her emotional reaction. "Cammy is watching her mother's YouTube vlog," she said in a hushed voice.

I felt my forehead wrinkle—a poker face is not my forte. "I don't understand."

"I've been an emotional wreck, and I'm trying so hard to lock up my emotions for Cammy's sake. May I?" she asked as she stood and dragged a chair from the corner of the room and placed it in front of me. This position placed her back toward Cammy, keeping her words and emotions hidden.

"Yes, great idea."

Cammy looked up, so I smiled and wiggled my fingertips at her in a subdued wave. Lindy turned around to blow her a kiss and coax her attention back to her iPad. It was then that I noticed the name tape on Cammy's blouse. It read Carter, but Porter was Lindy's last name.

"I brought Cammy so you could understand." She leaned forward. "You see, I'm a combat surgeon, and I lost Cammy's mom, Crystal Carter, when …" Lindy face-planted into the palms of her hands before she could finish the sentence. "I just can't get used to referring to Crystal in the past tense," she mumbled, muted by her hands.

"I'm here," I whispered.

Lindy looked up at me as she pulled tissues from the box and began blotting the tears that saturated the dark circles beneath her eyes. "I don't know what I was thinking when I put on mascara this morning." We both laughed.

She took a deep breath. "I was Crystal's surgeon. She died"—Lindy inhaled again and then exhaled with what sounded like one garbled word—"onmyoperatingtable." She took another deep breath and fixed her gaze on me. "Cammy is now my adopted daughter. She calls me Grams." Lindy rolled her eyes. "I'm too young for that name, I know …"

"Oh. My God." The words just carelessly slipped from my lips. "Not about 'Grams'—and yes, you are too young—but about you adopting her. Wow."

"I know, right?" She held tightly to the arms of the wooden chair.

"What you've done is so selfless and beautiful. I'm in awe." I searched her eyes. "How is Cammy doing?"

"Right now, she's watching her mama's deployment vlog." She blew her nose like a foghorn and then looked back at Cammy. We sat together in the abyss of her grief for several breaths.

Finally, I stood and approached Cammy. I leaned close and together we watched a lovely blonde Senior Airman making big-armed gestures and animated faces for her daughter's entertainment. Cammy sat giggling and looked up at me multiple times to gauge my reaction to her beautiful, silly mother. I wondered if she really understood that she would never see her mama again.

☆ ☆ ☆

Lindy shared that she was once married to a man ten years her senior. They wanted children so badly, but she was medically unable. She experienced too many miscarriages and more grief than one should have to bear. Her husband left her for a younger woman who could have children. This broke Lindy's heart in more ways than one, but she found her strength in the Lord and distraction in her work.

Lindy dedicated nearly thirty years of her life to becoming a trauma surgeon and had once been unshakeable in the operating room. Her medical career had been in full throttle until her last deployment, when she lost Crystal. She explained that when they met, Crystal became her shadow as she aspired to someday become a doctor. Lindy became a mother figure to this girl who grew up being tossed from one abusive foster family to the next. Crystal never felt wanted or loved—except by Jesus. She and Lindy shared a strong faith.

After losing Crystal, the mere sight of a scalpel sent Lindy into cold sweats and panic attacks, let alone trying to hold one. She needed to seek God for her next professional calling, but she hadn't yet; she was too frightened to learn what was around the corner.

Lindy also wrestled with how she had become Cammy's adoptive mother. At one point, she fought the idea that God may have orchestrated these events so she could have a child. In our second session, we explored Romans 8: "And we know that in all things God works for the good of those who love him " (v. 28). Lindy learned that God is never the author of travesty, hurt, and pain, yet when His believers are confronted by it, He finds a way to create good from the bad caused by Satan and our selfish nature. Once she understood the basic concept—if it's not love, it's not God—she was ready to begin the process of recovery.

Session 3

"Lindy, I want you to drift back to the most painful experience during that deployment. Do you think you can do that?" I asked.

"Yes," she replied as she dragged her sweaty palms across her thighs.

\<Rhythm Restoration\>

"Whoa," Lindy said as her eyes opened and darted back and forth across the room. She crisscrossed her arms, grasping her shoulders to ground herself in the chair. "I was right back there." She looked at me wide-eyed, placing her hand over her heart and taking long, deep breaths. "I was suffocated in all my battle rattle and the sirens were warning us of incoming rockets while I stood in the makeshift operating room, elbow deep in blood—someone's chest cavity."

Slowly, this incredible woman lifted her right hand and observed it trembling inches from her face. She shook her head and curled her fingers into a white-knuckled fist that she punched into her upper thigh.

"Be patient with yourself, Lindy. I believe you will gain control of your tremor once you're set free from your emotional pain."

She nodded her head and spread her fingers wide, releasing the tension. "May we continue?" I asked. She nodded again, her lips sealed in a straight line.

"Let's go back to that moment when you were elbow deep in someone's chest cavity."

<Rhythm Restoration>

"What did you experience?" I asked.

"Crystal. She's staring at me." She squeezed her eyes together tightly, conjuring up the image once more. "I can't look at her and operate at the same time." She raised one hand up to block the image. "I know she's looking at me for emotional support, but I can't give it right now. She's bleeding out; I need to work." She ran her fingers through her short, curly black hair. "I wish she'd stop looking at me." As she pounded the arms of the chair with both fists, an explosion of tears and snot flowed down her face. "Let's keep going. I gotta get through this part." Her legs bobbed up and down, as if she were trying to run from her nightmares only to remain stuck in place.

"Breathe, Lindy. Be thoughtful. Don't rush through the emotion like a charging bull. Sit with it." I emphasized my deep breaths to encourage her to follow my lead.

She sighed like an exasperated teenager, her chest fluttering with each inhalation and her lips quivering in protest of her tears. She opened her fists and sat palms up. She closed her eyes, inviting peace into her heart. Seconds passed and the tension in her face melted away.

"Now, are you ready?" She slowly nodded—demonstrating self-control. "All right, let's return to that image of Crystal's face."

<Rhythm Restoration>

"What did you experience?"

"My surgical tech clamps her artery while I strip off my battle rattle. I can't wear it because it hinders me. Let the f***ing rockets hit me. I'm not letting anything get in the way of this surgery." She tugged uncomfortably on her ACU blouse. "Ugh," she growled. She unbuttoned it and threw it to the floor. She then stood up, untucked her tan shirt, and waved it in and out for air. She sat back down in the chair and let out a weighted sigh. Her energy pulsed through the room, contrasting to a minute ago, when I was concerned that she was about to be swallowed up.

She closed her eyes and her hands came together to perform an imagined surgery. Her breathing slowed, but her hands involuntarily trembled in quick, rigid movements. "I'm trying to stop the bleeding but the bullet's exit hole through her stomach is too large." With eyes still closed, Lindy continued her intricate hand motions. It was like watching a real-life surgery in fast-forward. "Sh**. There's not enough time, and she's losing all the transfused blood we're pumping into her."

Frustrated, Lindy dropped her shaky hands into her lap—defeated. "She's flatlining." Lindy's fists tightened as if holding defibrillators. "All clear." Lindy said it with vigor in her voice. "All clear." Her voice softened. "All clear," she whispered. Lindy covered her eyes with her hands, and tears poured out from between her fingers, and down her forearms. The surgeon's hands were crying.

"I can't believe I forgot that moment." She stared off into the distance. "I closed Crystal's bright-blue eyes. They looked like sapphires in contrast to her pale white face, but they were empty because she was gone. I couldn't bear to see them go gray." Once her mind turned the silence into deafening noise, she shook her head, as if she could simply shake off the feeling. "Let's keep going."

"One last time, let's return to that hurtful experience and see if there is anything you may have left out."

<Rhythm Restoration>

"What did you experience?" I asked.

"The moment they rushed Crystal into the trauma bay." Lindy's well of tears was drained and emptied. "I ran to the litter and took her hand. 'I can't die, Mama,' she said. She called me Mama because she said I was the closest to a mother figure she ever had. Then I did something I never should've done: I promised her that it would all be okay."

Her breaths were quick and heavy. Behind Lindy's eyes, the thoughts were ricocheting like stray bullets in her mind. "You see, Crystal worked in aircraft maintenance. As quick reaction force, she was called to recover survivors and critical equipment from a downed Osprey. But as her squad approached the crash site, they got caught in an ambush and Crystal was shot." Lindy massaged her jaw; she had been clenching her teeth in each moment that passed without words.

"You have deep regret for promising Crystal that it would be okay," I said. She nodded and avoided eye contact with me. "Let's hold that thought and come back to it," I said. "The good news is that we're done going back to that moment. You've done an excellent job confronting your fear.

"Now we're going to go somewhere different. I want you to visualize all the ways God was present with you throughout that deployment.

He never left you, and He never left Crystal. Remember, He is not the author of your hurt. His presence can come in the form of love in the midst of darkness. Do you think you can visualize God's presence throughout that time?" I asked.

"Yes," she replied as she immediately closed her eyes and fell into a slow and consistent tapping rhythm.

<Rhythm Restoration>

"What did you experience?" I asked.

I want you to visualize all the ways God was present with you throughout that deployment.

"When I first met Crystal at the DFAC, she said, 'Ma'am, I'm going to be a doctor someday too. I'm Crystal, by the way.' She extended her hand, blocking me from my bowl of oatmeal. I shook it, and I said, 'Nice to meet you, Crystal-someday-doctor. Want to join me?'"

Lindy acted the whole scene out, caught her breath, and continued. "So she sat down and spoke to me as if we'd been age-old friends. Crystal talked about her job in aircraft maintenance, her life goals—obviously becoming a doctor—and of course, her daughter." Lindy's head fell down, and she sank more deeply into her seat and into reality.

Then a smile began to spread across her face and a laugh bubbled up from her chest as she slowly lifted her head. "Crystal told me that Cammy was half black and that she needed serious help with managing textured hair and ashy skin. And most importantly, she wondered if she needed to apply sunscreen to her daughter."

We both laughed.

"You see, Crystal hovered around me, almost as soon as my boots hit the ground at Bagram Air Base. She was big into 'energy.' Crystal was a crystal collector; she loved crystals—no pun intended. She'd ordered them online by bulk. She believed my energy was powerful and it would somehow effervesce through her and magically make her a doctor. She would coordinate her schedule with mine—DFAC, gym, breaks—you name it. If our schedules permitted, she was my shadow—my stalker." Lindy laughed. "Cammy has her mother's persistence."

She placed her hand on her forehead and shook her head. "God, help me," she pleaded toward the ceiling. "But in all seriousness, it was no doubt that the Lord placed her in my life to soften my hardened heart."

"How beautiful, a divine connection. You also played an incredible role in her life," I said. Lindy wiped away a tear.

"I want you to continue to recognize the presence of God through-out that deployment, and whenever you're ready, I want you to fall into your own rhythm …"

<Rhythm Restoration>

"What did you experience?" I asked.

"Crystal begged me to join in a video chat with Cammy. She said it was important for her daughter to be surrounded by strong women, especially women of color."

Lindy touched a glistening ray of sun that shone brightly on the office wall. She placed her hand in the light and watched it hit each of her fingers. Interestingly, her tremor was not present. "It was the first time I visited her bunk. Tiny rainbows came to life in a land of darkness where no light should shine. They danced on her plywood walls—originating from a small, multifaceted crystal she hung in her window. She said God was light and the best way for her to see Him was through the reflections of her precious stones—and in Cammy's eyes." I nodded, eager to learn more of her story. "It always shocked me that a girl who experienced so much childhood misfortune loved God so intensely and saw His reflection in all His creations."

"I imagine that she loved God so much because He never abandoned her. God was responsible for all the good that transpired in her life—never the bad," I said.

"You're so right." Lindy looked out the window. "Crystal and Cammy were chatterboxes—pinging off each other's superpowered energy." Lindy demonstrated their interaction with two hands that she used like sock puppets.

"I can only imagine," I replied.

Lindy laughed and clapped her hands together. "Crystal's best friend, Jenna, cared for Cammy when she was deployed. Crystal would buy small duplicate gifts for Cammy, so she could pretend to pass these gifts through the computer screen to Jenna, who would then hand them off to Cammy. It was like magic! She passed sparkly trinkets and gems through the screen and it amused Cammy to no end. Crystal had a way of making everything special—truly a magical touch."

"Wow. Now that's creative!" I replied.

"Incredible. Another God-inspired moment in the middle of such darkness," Lindy said as she smeared tears of joy across her cheeks.

"I'm so glad you have beautiful memories like that to share with Cammy as she grows older." Lindy looked out the window. "Are you ready to continue?"

"Yes." We both situated ourselves in our seats, almost as if to strap in for the next ride.

"Now we're going to switch it up again. I want you to visualize how God used you as a vessel of His love and grace for others, an extension of Himself."

<Rhythm Restoration>

"What did you experience?" I asked.

"This is definitely a first," she said, smiling and looking out the window at the sky. "I visualized Jesus next to me in the operating room. He was bracing me with His hands on my shoulders," she said as tears ran down her cheeks. "I did my best to be His hands, His feet, His words, and His heart ... and there were miracles on that operating table—there's no doubt about it." Lindy wiped her drippy nose. "He allowed me to do incredible things to save lives, but there were also times when it was not possible ..." Her eyes widened. "But it went beyond surgery ... He used me as a vessel to be a mother figure to Crystal and some others. There were young surgical techs that I counseled during our losses. I didn't intend to, but they came to me, and I spoke to them about God and explained to them that this life goes well beyond the flesh—that sometimes we can't save the flesh, and when that happens, the spirit returns home to Jesus." She blotted her eyes. "My goodness, I need to practice what I preach and believe those words with conviction. The surg techs and Crystal followed me to chapel every Sunday. We were blessed to have one another. What did you say earlier? Divine connections? That's exactly what they were."

"What a beautiful realization, Lindy." I swallowed hard to stop the lump from forming in my throat. "Earlier you spoke about the times you were unable to save lives. I want you to visualize where God was when you lost the patients you couldn't save ..."

"All right," she replied as she took a deep breath and began to tap quickly.

<Rhythm Restoration>

"What did you experience?" I asked.

"I don't know why I didn't see it sooner, but our Lord was with them the entire time. He never left them. Jesus never left Crystal. In fact, as Jesus had His hands on my shoulders, Crystal was looking past me at Him. Oh my … what a thing to realize. He was her comforter. She's with Him now."

"Amen," I replied. "Remember, you promised Crystal that it would all be okay? Was it okay?" I asked.

"More than okay," she replied with a wide smile. "There's no better place to be than in the presence of our Lord. Even Cammy is well taken care of. She will want for nothing in her life, thanks to Him. I kept my promise to Crystal," Lindy said, shocked at her realization. She looked out the window and whispered to the heavens, "I kept my promise."

I reached for the pen across my desk and handed it to Lindy. "Will you please hold it up?" I asked. Lindy held the pen vertically from the base, two feet from the middle of her nose. "That's your scalpel." Just the thought of it worsened her tremor. "Now, go back to that image of Jesus laying His hands on you as you operate." Her tremor began to slow. "Breathe in slowly and repeat after me, 'I can do all things through Christ,' now exhale slowly, 'who is my strength.'" We repeated this confession several times. Her well of tears replenished and watered her cheeks as her hand steadied. "Open your eyes. What do you see?" I asked.

"Oh my God," Lindy replied. She kept her "scalpel" perfectly still.

I placed my clipboard in front of her. "I want you to draw one large circle on this sheet of white paper." Without hesitation and in one swoop, Lindy drew a perfect freehand circle. I was stunned; I didn't expect it to be that good. "I want you to draw another circle inside it and keep going until it feels right to stop."

Lindy's hand was free of tremors and each circle was absolutely perfect—unbelievable. Once finished, she threw the pen down onto the clipboard. She was completely awestruck by what she had drawn. She pointed to the largest circle first and said, "God." Then she pointed to the next largest circle, "Me." Next, "Crystal." And the smallest circle, "Cammy." She inhaled long and deep, and said, "We are in His infinite love, and they are in mine."

☆ ☆ ☆

Session 6

"I want you to go find Crystal now, wherever you imagine her to be. Do you think you can do that?" I asked.

Lindy nodded as she blotted tears from her cheeks.

<Rhythm Restoration>

"What did you experience?" I asked.

"Crystal. She sat next to me on a bench in a beautiful garden. She took both her hands in mine. 'You need these hands,' she said." Lindy raised her hands to examine them, and tears glided down her cheeks. "She told me, 'You need to love Cammy with those hands, and you need to continue to heal us with them too.'" She quickly shook her head, as if to shake off her thoughts, and asked, "Is what I'm experiencing normal, Doc?" A curtain of tears fell down her face and onto her ACU blouse.

"It is, Lindy. Most combat vets experience healing images like this. But I noticed that you prayed before you began. Is that correct?"

"Yes." She reached for the tissue box.

"Well, that's your answer," I replied.

"I want to tell Crystal something. Is that crazy?" Lindy smeared the tears across her face. "I've learned my lesson: no mascara when I see you, Doc." We both smiled.

"Stop judging yourself, Lindy. Of course it's not crazy. Go on and tell her."

"Okay," she replied as she grabbed a tissue to mop up her tears. Without any prompting, she immediately began tapping to a slow and relaxed rhythm.

<Rhythm Restoration>

"I'm so sorry I couldn't save you." Lindy fell into her own orbit as she stared out the window.

I waited about a minute before I asked, "Did she respond?"

"Yes, she did." She shook her head in disbelief of her experience. "Crystal said, '*Sorry* is not a word that I know any longer, not here, because here we only see the good in your heart.' She told me how grateful she was for the love that I"—Lindy broke out the air quotations—"'poured into her' when I tried to save her. Crystal said, 'I was filled with your love in my last breath.' She proceeded to tell me that there's nothing wrong with death and that I will save the lives I'm meant to save." Lindy looked at me. "She's alive in the Spirit." Her breaths were thoughtful—long and drawn out—as she focused on the centering of her own spirit.

"I would like to make peace with the others I lost." She closed her eyes and began tapping.

<Rhythm Restoration>

"Crystal physically turned my head with her hands," Lindy said as she softly touched her cheeks, trying to evoke that sensation, "and there they were, all those I lost on the operating table. All of them in white—intact and whole, healthy and full and, most importantly, at peace. I stood up and told them, 'I'm so sorry.'" She reached for the distance, her eyes shut as her mind conjured up the last image. Tears rolled down her face, reflecting the sunlight. "Thank You, Jesus. I see Him standing beside them. He never left them." With her eyes still shut, she pointed to their faces, one by one—almost a dozen. Lindy opened her eyes in search of mine. "They bowed their heads and faded away." She shook her head in awe and disbelief. "Then I turned to Crystal, but she was gone too."

☆ ☆ ☆

Final Session

As we walked down the hallway to my office, Lindy leaned close and whispered into my ear. "Today Cammy decided to retire the uniform. She did it all on her own. She even put it in the washing machine—a small miracle that can't go unnoticed." We both chuckled.

I turned to Cammy and reached for her free hand. "Tell me about the cool outfit you're wearing today, Cammy."

"Well, I'm a doctor. Isn't that obvious?"

"It is! But what kind of doctor?"

"A cardiothoracic surgeon." She pronounced each syllable with enthusiasm. It boggled my mind hearing such a big word come from such a small child. Cammy whipped out a real stethoscope and showed it off as if it were a pink-feathered boa around her neck.

Lindy prepared a spot on the floor for Cammy to entertain herself.

When Lindy was ready, I asked, "How have you been since I saw you last?"

"I decided to take time away from surgery," she said, straight to the point. My heart sank. Had she given into the insecurities and doubt? "I haven't finished my sentence yet." I didn't realize my face was betraying my thoughts. I smiled and shook my head. "I am taking time away from surgery to …" She let the word linger, teasing me with the suspense.

"To what, already?" I asked, and we both laughed.

"To train other surgeons on tactical surgical skills needed to save more lives in combat. In garrison, we're not taught on victims with such traumatic wounds. Thankfully, that doesn't happen enough in America for surgeons to effectively get the experience they'll need while overseas. I've proposed a plan to the USAF, and I named the course Surgical Life Support Training.

"This is my way of taking it slow and making peace. I don't know if I want to deploy again—that's still an unanswered question. The itch that compelled me to return to the Sandbox isn't as strong as it once was. It was more about the adrenaline addiction and the obsessive-compulsive need to make amends for every failed surgery by saving ten lives for each one I lost. I can't be mad at myself for what I didn't know or learn prior to my first surgical deployment. But I can pay it forward with the knowledge I've acquired. I want to share it with others so they can save more lives."

Chapter 8

YOU IN EXCHANGE FOR ME

Emari is a fictional character whose emotional experiences accurately reflect those of many combat veterans.

Name:	Emari Booysen
Gender:	Male
Age:	34
Ethnicity:	Kenyan American
Branch / Rank:	USAF / SSgt
Time in Service:	10 years
Military Occupation:	Security Forces
Deployments:	2; Iraq

I walked along the shoreline, where the black ocean met the white sand and relentlessly sucked at my combat boots with each step. The moon lit up the entire beach that night. My muscles quivered and my bones floated somewhere in my flesh after a ten-mile ruck march in the Florida sunshine. I hadn't slept in nearly forty-eight hours. This was only the third day of the vigorous selection and assessment for special operations; the worst was yet to come.

Although the salty ocean air saturated my lungs and the humidity threatened to suffocate me, I slowed each breath I took to synchronize with the rise and fall of the tide. Standing here was the only way I would recharge—spiritually and physically. Carried away in the magnificence of God's creation, I lifted my hands to pray.

Lord, please fill me with Your Holy Spirit, and cast healing over my aching body. I pray for Your strength, guidance, and the words to help heal others. Please allow me to be Your vessel, and let Your glory shine through me. Amen.

I brought my hands down and lifted my head to take in one last moment of solitude before the chaos would erupt.

As I stood mesmerized by the ocean, the jarring sound of my phone alarm sent an electric shock through my body. It was time to raid the candidates' barrack at 2400 hours. These were the guys who wanted to be *the guys*: Air Force Special Forces—more specifically, pararescue jumpers. Better known as PJs, they would rescue and medically treat downed military personnel, often while operating in hostile areas. These highly trained specialists not only provide combat support but are skilled parachutists, scuba divers, rock climbers, and even Arctic-trained to save lives wherever and whenever needed. My mission was to determine if they were psychologically fit to become part of the elite rescuing force.

One-third of the twelve candidates had already rung the bell of defeat. The other one-third would be eliminated by us: psychologists and cadre (trainers). Of the four selectees, only one or two would make it through the three-year pipeline to proudly wear the maroon beret.

I ran up the beach to the old barrack. There was a noticeable sense of lightness in my movement and warmth in my veins. God was certainly present, but someone else was watching.

Training Day: One of Five

The tiny room felt sterile and uncomfortable with its fluorescent lighting, plain white walls, and concrete floors. My purpose in attending was to stir the candidates—provoke them—see if they'd emotionally crack under the pressure of rapid-fire questions that tugged at their weak spots. I sat stiffly in my dress blue uniform, but maintaining a stoic and expressionless bearing during our interviews was incongruent with my typically colorful and animated personality.

Emari formally reported to his interview, also in his dress blues. He was a giant. It practically broke my neck to look at him when we stood to greet each other. You'd never guess that he was the oldest of all the candidates by ten years. This Airman was the underdog because of it.

Emari had an Afrikaans accent. Words that ended in *-er* had a soft *ah* sound, and they smoothly and eloquently rolled off his full lips. His smile was bright white, especially in contrast to his deep mocha-colored skin. He was a natural performer with a charisma that could captivate most people, but without a hint of narcissism. Instead, he was full of humility and gratitude.

"Emari, tell me about your childhood," I began.

He shifted in his seat and placed his hands flatly on his lap. He looked down at his reflection in the distorted metal table. "It was an adventure," he said as he looked up at me. "I didn't know if I'd survive from one day to the next."

Emari tightly clasped his hands together. "I'm sure you know, but I was born and raised in a rural location near South Africa." I nodded. "I was the only child to my motha and fatha. We lived in a beautiful village. It was peaceful and everyone was like family." He wiped his hands across the tops of his pants. "But on a terrible day, a rebel army invaded our village and burned it to the ground." He drew in a long breath of air. "They kidnapped me and the other boys. We were to become children soldiez. The captors took us far, far away. To this day, I don't know where. But we arrived at a campsite." He wiped the sweat from his forehead.

"To make a very long story short, my fatha found me a month lata. The rebel leada instructed me to kill him with my machine gun." Emari steeled himself by searching for his reflection on the metal tabletop, a distraction to stifle his emotion. "Of course, I did not. My fatha told me to run and so I did.

"They tried to shoot me and then chased afta me, but they did not catch me. The odds were strangely in my fava." Emari shook his head. "I know they killed my fatha. I'm certain of it. I heard the gunshots from high in the tree that I climbed. I stayed there for three days, waiting for the army to relocate." Emari shifted in his seat. "I drifted from village to village doing hard laba to earn my keep until I found my motha two years lata. It was insane that I found ha. Again, what were the chances?" He shook his head. "She was sold as a slave to anotha village, but ha owna treated ha kindly. I was so grateful for that man." He took a deep breath as if he were inhaling fresh air after a rainstorm.

"That must've been an incredible reunion," I commented.

"It was the most beautiful moment of my entira life." To keep the tears at bay, he quickly picked up his water bottle and chugged. "My motha's owna was the one who guided me to the military. I owe him everything. I have my American citizenship because of him, and my motha is my dependent. We are very blessed." Emari clasped both his hands together and bowed his head, almost in prayer.

"I agree." We both smiled. I could only begin to imagine the tragedy he had seen throughout his life, not including his two deployments to Iraq. I was sitting before a true warrior. "Tell me, why do you want to become a PJ?" I asked.

"I know. I am an old man, right? Probably much olda than you, even." He laughed gently and placed both hands in his lap. "I had my motha color my gray hairs. I'm not kidding you." He ran his fingers atop his nearly bald head. We both laughed.

I didn't tell you the entire story. I was afraid it would make me seem crazy.

"I am here on behalf of my brotha, SrA Kent." Emari's smile quickly vanished as he took in a stiff breath and stared beyond me, almost mesmerized. He was distracted for a moment but then redirected his focus to me. It seemed as though he was trying to avoid looking at whatever he saw behind me. "SrA Kent was the medic attached to our Security Forces flight in Iraq, and he saved my life." He stayed very quiet and still for several moments. His gaze never returned to that spot.

"Did you get wounded? And he patched you up?" I needed to keep the momentum going. I sat with a candidate every hour on the hour; no time to get stuck.

"I wish it were that," he said, looking directly at me. "Kent caught several bullets for me." Emari pursed his lips together. "I killed the insurgent who shot him and then rendered aid to Kent, but he was gone—dead before I could do anything." He shook his head and quickly sipped more water. "He wanted nothing more than to be a PJ. So, I'm gonna live the dream out, to honor my brotha." He smiled at me. "Of course, with your blessing, Ma'am." Emari bowed his head.

Training Day: Two of Five

When I wasn't conducting psychological assessments or interviews, I observed the candidates' behaviors. *Were they team players? How did they manage their frustrations? Did they give up quickly? What were their problem-solving styles?* At times, I observed by participating in the events, like the ruck march on the beach.

We assembled for this day's event at the outdoor pool and the wave machine. Along the side of the pool was a dugout for the purpose of underwater observation, similar to watching fish in an aquarium—a bit voyeuristic. One of the candidate requirements was to see how many laps they could complete fully immersed with their legs tied together (like mermen without fins). The recruits swam in their long-sleeved camouflage uniform, a winter-weight cloth that promoted sinking once saturated.

Initially, Emari was on a roll until he suddenly slowed down. I was concerned that he'd be the first to give up. As he was about to resurface in defeat, something confusing happened that I can't explain. Ascending to the surface, he was suddenly pulled back down into the water by what seemed to be a force, but nothing was there. Emari seemed caught off guard, excessively flapping his legs for a moment. I ran up the stairs to signal for help, but then he recovered and continued to propel himself across the pool—completely unfazed—as if nothing had happened. I was the only below-deck observer and likely the only one who noticed this situation, unseen to the cadres watching from above. Since this was my first assessment and selection, I chalked it up to nothing more than a strong pool current caused by the other swimmers.

Training Day: Three of Five

Several leadership activities challenged the candidates to use their problem-solving skills, and Emari always stood out as the natural leader. The younger Airmen looked to him for his calm and calculated guidance; he was the glue that held his team together.

In the suffocating humidity and penetrating sunshine, the candidates partook in a boat exercise. The first part required the team to row out into a croc-infested lake and rescue dozens of drowning dummies. The second part, while on land, required the teams to hold the empty three-hundred-pound boats above their heads (six men per boat) to be the last team standing.

The lake was a murky brown surrounded by swamp vegetation and lurking eyes. We had weapons on standby should the swamp creatures become violent. I had to douse myself in extra-strength bug repellent to avoid getting eaten alive by mosquitos the size of butterflies. The candidates didn't have the luxury of using either topical ointments or painkillers.

The teams had three minutes to come up with a battle plan and then execute it. Before Emari even opened his mouth, the candidates immediately encircled him to receive his direction. He suggested they spread themselves out in a grid and hand the dummy bodies to the next person closest to the boat—all while treading putrid swamp water. One candidate would remain on the boat to load the bodies. Emari asked for feedback and ideas from his team—all of which he integrated into their battle plan.

The other teams took a different approach that resulted in too much chaos and lost time. Emari's team performed flawlessly.

During the second part, Emari held up the middle of the boat, toward the right side. His other teammates were spread out to distribute the weight. At one point, his entire team collapsed to the ground, and Emari was left standing alone with the boat. The cadre beside me stood in disbelief at his ability to continue to hold this three-hundred-pound boat over his head, appearing to defy the laws of gravity. After about ten seconds of holding the boat alone—knees and legs violently trembling—another teammate recovered and returned to help to carry his burden. Everyone gathered around Emari in disbelief as they shouted and hollered with excitement, applauding his incredible strongman feat.

Training Day: Four of Five

Bloody boots were everywhere from ripped-off toenails and heel blisters that became chunks of ripped skin. Over the past few days, the candidates physically performed more than fifty miles of ruck marching, physical training tests, swimming, CrossFit, and so much more, not to include all the mental gymnastics we put them through.

In full battle gear, the candidates partook in their umpteenth CrossFit session, but this time with mouthfuls of sand and saltwater that crept into every crevice; wounds were set on fire. Their physical pain and suffering were incongruent with the beautiful shoreline landscape—the perfect backdrop for a wedding or a romantic stroll on the beach. The glorious sunset looked like a melting bar of gold, and a cool and gentle breeze pulsed through the air.

The candidates had no time to appreciate the beauty around them as they dove in and out of the ocean—swimming and low-crawling on the shore. They dragged each other's limp bodies out of the cold waters and across the beach, simulating real-life rescue scenarios. Just when they thought they couldn't possibly be smoked anymore, the cadre forced them to line up in a row—shoulder to shoulder—to perform flutter kicks as the tide threatened to wash them away.

While shouting cadence, Emari continually turned to look to his right as if someone or something were there, but he was at the end of the line. Some of us noticed this unusual behavior, but we chalked it up to an attempt to alleviate a side cramp. I figured it was something more, but I didn't question it because I wanted him to persevere. Perhaps I should've checked in.

All was forgotten after the grand finale: sugar cookies! The Airmen were commanded to toss heaps of sand all over their bodies; they were the sugar cookies. The joke was on them.

Training Day: Five of Five

The one-story barrack was spotless. Each of the remaining candidates had only one duffle bag placed neatly at the foot of his cot, and beside it, a pair of damp and musty combat boots. They slept head to toe in three rows of cots that spread across the room. By now, most of the cots were empty; each vacancy occurred after the ring of *that* bell.

At zero dark thirty, the cadre brutally woke up the candidates with eardrum-bursting sirens and high-pitched whistles. Startled faces sprang from cots across the large barren room. The Airmen frantically pulled their battle uniforms over their PT clothes and fumbled to lace up their combat boots—except one.

Emari appeared calm and collected. He sat on his cot and made no effort to get dressed. Instead, he slowly walked out the door with the cadre shouting mere inches from his face. He approached the rusted bell that hung from the roof outside the barrack. As Emari reached for the leather strap that would end his candidacy, I ran up to him and gestured with my hand for him to stop. No amount of noise I made could compete with the cacophony of chaos in that moment. He looked at me and shook his head.

Once dressed, Airmen poured outside the barracks to watch in disbelief as Emari stood milliseconds from surrendering his dream. As his fingertips pinched the leather strap, I stood firm, hands on hips, and I glared up at him. Finally, the noise stopped as the suspense narrowed in on us.

"Stop! Come with me," I commanded in my most officer-like voice.

"Yes, Ma'am," he replied, removing his hand from the leather strap. He did an about-face turn and caught up with me. At his height, Emari only needed to take two long strides to close the almost ten-foot distance between us.

"Let's go sit on the beach for minute," I said as I pointed to the shore where the sun was barely beginning to rise. The horizon was an ombre blue, separated by a thin orange line that kissed the top of the ocean and the bottom of the sky.

I collapsed onto the sand, muscles too sore to sit down gracefully. I couldn't even begin to imagine how Emari's body was feeling. "So, what's going on? Why ring the bell?" I asked in a no-bullsh** tone.

"With all due respect, Ma'am, if I truthfully answa your question, it will be the equivalent of me ringing the bell anyway. Is that what you want?" he asked in a gentle voice.

"Emari, not all answers are always black and white," I replied.

"I suppose not. If anyone could understand my experience, it would be you." He stared at the glistening waters. The sun now looked like a bright-white yoke spilling onto the vast ocean.

"Why do you say that?" I asked. Immediately, I felt defensive.

"I saw you," he said. Emari looked at me. "I saw you praying," he finished his sentence.

My heart stopped, and I didn't know what to think. "All right," I replied.

"I slipped out to pray too, at that exact time, but you wa there seeming to be in perfect harmony with the universe as you lifted your hands to praise the Lord." He looked out at the ocean and pointed to where I had stood that night.

"I'd never interrupt that." He turned to me and said, "Seeing you there strengthened my faith in that moment, so I chose to carry on and not give up on this calling. But now I …" His words trailed off into silence.

Seeing you there strengthened

my faith in that moment, so

I chose to carry on and not

give up on this calling.

"Time is not on our side. Please, I want to understand. Why are you quitting, Emari?"

"Because I'm pissed off at God." His brows fell together into one solitary line across his forehead.

"He took Kent from you?" I suggested.

"Yes, exactly." He dug his bare feet into the sand. "I didn't tell you the entira story. I was afraid it would make me seem crazy. But f*** it. I have nothing to lose now."

"Please, go on," I replied.

"Well, the day before he took the bullets on my behalf, some crazy sh** went down." Emari hugged his knees. "We were on a recon mission in a village. Kent was standing on a wall with three othas, pulling security above the rest of us. When we were done gathering the intel we needed, I shouted to Kent that we were rolling out. He couldn't hear me down below, so he took a knee to lean in, and just as he did, a snipa round whizzed past his ear, burning the side of his helmet." Emari cupped his right ear with his hand. "We all took cover and made our way out. But if I had not called to him at that very moment, and if he had not taken a knee to hear me, he'd be dead—shot through the gut."

"Why does this make you angry?" I asked.

"Because I had been answering all sorts of questions that Kent had about God since the beginning of that deployment. He wanted to become a believa. He said it was the only thing that brought him peace." He shook his head. "Afta that near miss, he said it was a miracle and that he believed with all of his heart." He took in a slow and labored breath. "He had no more questions for me. He asked if I would escort him to the Chaplain for a quick baptism." Emari pushed out a half laugh. "It was like a Vegas marriage but to God." He laughed harder, but he stopped because his muscle contractions were too painful. "So of course, I went to his shotgun baptism!" Emari snapped his fingers to demonstrate how quickly it happened.

No matter how hard he tried to let humor dominate this part of the conversation, it just wouldn't work. He looked at the bright rays of light and then let his head drop. He smashed his palms into his face and dragged them across his eyes and cheeks, smearing away his tears. "Afta his baptism, Kent said he would become a PJ to save more lives to do God's calling to an even greata degree." Emari bit his lower lip. "I gotta stop feeling like I'm emotionally battling God," he replied.

"You couldn't battle God if you wanted," I replied. We both let a small laugh erupt.

"But why did God take him from me? Especially afta he was baptized?" asked Emari.

"God isn't responsible for death, nor is He responsible for the evil in the world, Emari. *We* are. Our selfish nature causes us to do terrible things. It goes all the way back to Adam and Eve. God gifted us with free will so we may experience a loving relationship with Him. God will never take that away, no matter how terrible our decisions are. But the most important thing is that we cast our focus on the blessing of our eternal life through Christ and not get stuck on the earthly things. Was it God or the enemy who selfishly chose to take Kent?" I asked.

"The enemy. I neva looked at it like that."

I allowed several moments for him to process those words. "Kent chose to be your body shield, correct?"

Emari nodded, and tears broke free like a river.

"He saved your life, but you saved his first," I said.

"What do you mean by that?"

"Spiritually, you were a huge part of how he came to know God. He became a believer because of how you carried yourself. You were probably the closest to Christ that he had ever seen." I smiled at him. "John 15:13 says, 'There is no greater love than to lay down one's life for one's friends'" (NLT). I looked intently at Emari. "And where there is love, there is God. Kent's love for you was a reflection of God, and for that you are blessed."

"Damn. I neva saw it like that." He stared off at the breathtaking sunrise.

"Close your eyes, Emari. I want you to visualize Kent and imagine where he is right now."

Tears rolled down his cheeks as he held his face toward the warmth of the rising sun. In the golden light his cheeks glistened, and he didn't bother to wipe his tears. After about a minute, Emari opened his eyes and said, "Kent is in the sunrise—a new beginning. He's healthy and happy. I know it's crazy, but I saw him doing butterfly kicks beside me in the ocean. He held me up. And now he's telling me to stop being a damn crybaby. He's got my six." Emari laughed.

"Amen," I replied.

"Doc, I gotta be honest, but this past week I've been in the presence of something strange." The words spilled quickly from his lips. "There's been this faint warm glow around me. It has no shape or origin; it just exists. It appears every time I'm ready to throw in the towel." Emari wiped the beads of sweat that formed at his brow.

"What does it feel like?" I asked.

"Pure peace. I'm reenergized. I have strength. I have purpose. I feel it now."

"What do you believe it is?" I asked.

"None otha than the Holy Spirit," Emari replied.

"That explains everything I saw …" I pieced it all together—the times I witnessed Emari do incredible feats or zone out in the midst of his physical assessments.

"You noticed?" he asked.

"We all did. The Holy Spirit doesn't show off subtly," I said, and we both laughed.

"You know, God led me to you by showing me I could trust you when I saw you praying, and He placed you here right now to put me in my place." Emari rubbed his eyes with his fingertips.

"You're right. Get back to your troops, SSgt!"

Murder Board

We sat in the freezing cold war room at the headquarters building. A dozen of us gathered around a long, glossy cherrywood table with plush blue carpet sprawled out beneath our feet. In the middle of the table was a pitcher of ice water that would never melt. Pictures of warriors arrayed the walls. Everyone sat poised in dress blues.

This was the murder board. The team brutally evaluated every remaining candidate on each aspect of his performance—from psychological assessments to swimming. Peer reviews were read aloud as part of the 360-degree assessment. In the end, everyone had a say in who stayed or left.

"Capt. Tajiri, what happened with SSgt Booysen?" asked the Air Force Special Operations Colonel (psychologist). He was an older man with silver hair and leathery, tanned skin. The Colonel looked like he had just stepped out of an action-packed military movie.

"Sir," I replied. "He was experiencing a moment of grief." The Colonel grunted. "His wingman saved his life while on deployment in Iraq last year, Sir. But sadly, this hero ended up passing immediately after his act of heroism. His wingman's most esteemed goal was to become a PJ. As you can imagine, this is why SSgt Booysen aspired to pursue this calling at his older age. This morning, he felt unworthy of the success he had experienced thus far and experienced a fleeting moment of survivor's guilt." I sat taller and straighter.

"Should we be concerned about a diagnosis of PTSD?" the Colonel asked sternly.

"No, Sir. He just never saw himself making it as far as he did during the assessment process, Sir." Heads nodded all around the table. "I provided supportive counseling, and that seemed to help, Sir. From a behavioral health perspective, I find him fit for the PJ training pipeline."

"All right, Capt. I take your word for it."

Truly, I thought I'd have to work harder to defend Emari. But I didn't have to; God had his six.

The cadre spent at least two minutes recalling Emari's superman feat: holding the boat over his head all by himself. Emari's call sign became "Super Ol' Man."

The Selection Results

I returned to the claustrophobic interview room to disseminate the results. One at a time, the candidates received the news from their assigned psychologist. I had already informed three candidates as to why they would not be advancing. Emari was the last to receive his results.

He cleaned up nicely and presented in his dress blues—the only candidate who elected to do so. I requested he take a seat.

"Looking sharp after a week in the trenches. How do you feel?" I asked.

"Like a million dollas, Ma'am," he replied, trying to hold back his smile.

"Do you think you can do this crazy, intense mission without the grace of God?" I asked.

He looked confused. "Is that a trick question, Ma'am?" Emari massaged his chin with his index finger and thumb.

"Should it be?" I asked in return.

"No. I cannot do this or anything else without God's good grace."

"Well, I'm sorry to inform you"—I paused. Emari looked down and away—"but your mission has become infinitely more challenging as a PJ recruit."

Chapter 9

YOUR BLOOD ON
MY HANDS

Wendy is a fictional character whose emotional experiences accurately reflect those of many combat veterans.

Name:	Wendy Cooper
Gender:	Female
Age:	32
Ethnicity:	Caucasian
Branch / Rank:	Army / MAJ
Time in Service:	15 years
Military Occupation:	Air Defense Artillery Officer
Deployments:	4; Iraq and Afghanistan

Session 1

"Do you mind if I take off my shoes?" Wendy asked, having already begun untying her shoelaces. She didn't look up or wait for my response before she tugged at the heel of her black workout shoes. Wendy had spent the morning doing her own PT: running eight miles at zero dark thirty. I later discovered that running, smoking Virginia Slims, midnight walks, and hours of painting were the only activities that brought her temporary solace.

"Um, sure!" I replied, a little surprised.

Wendy adjusted her socks, pulling one over a tattoo of a white flower, just one of many tattoos that reflected how she viewed the world.

"Sorry," she said, looking up at me as she folded up her legs and crossed them.

"No need to be sorry. Mi office es su office," I replied, and we both gave a half-hearted laugh.

Wendy tucked bright-red strands of hair behind her ears, a stark contrast to her pale face. She looked older than her age, with dark circles under her eyes and leathery skin that had borne the intense summer heat of four deployments in the Sandbox—sometimes Iraq, sometimes Afghanistan.

She reached for the blanket draped over the sofa and pulled it over her legs. "I figure that's what it's here for," she said, rubbing her long, calloused fingers on the velvety blanket. "It feels so nice." Wendy's nails were chewed to the quick, raw and fleshy pink.

"I want you to feel comfortable," I said as I rolled my chair closer to her.

She looked up at me with large, hazel-green eyes and then returned to preoccupying her fingertips with the blanket texture. A solitary tear escaped the corner of her eye and slid down her cheek onto her raw lips. Then the floodgates opened, and rivers of tears poured over her faded freckles and onto her PT uniform.

"Wendy, what are those tears for?" I asked gently.

She hid behind the canopy of her red hair and whispered, "My brother died, twice." She closed her eyes to wipe her tears.

I knew her words were carefully chosen. Before I met Wendy, her commander told me she was the most gifted officer he had come across in his career and that she had the potential to advance to become a general officer if she "got her act together."

"Tell me more," I said, eager to learn her perspective.

"Well, you know they redeployed me (brought me home) because I lost my sh**, right?" she asked, her words inflected to a higher pitch. Finally, she gave me a steady gaze.

"I know that much," I said. I knew why she had returned a month earlier than the rest of her troops, but I wanted to hear her side of the story—uncontaminated by the gossip.

"Well, about two weeks ago, they found me sprawled on top of my specialist's dead body, screaming someone else's name," she said. She laughed with irritation and shook her head at her own ridiculousness. "They thought I was screwing around with a teenager because of how distraught I was. Then for a hot minute they thought I had killed him." She shoved back the blanket and began scratching her legs, and long red streaks appeared up and down her white shins. "If I was a man, do you think I'd be accused of that sh**?" she asked.

"That sounds awful," I replied as I shook my head.

"Well, it's neither here nor there. They're just rumors," she said as she wiped the trail of mucous that dripped from her nose like a yo-yo with every breath.

"They are just rumors, yes. But I imagine it feels like so much more than rumors, especially with how much you've invested in the Army and, most importantly, in your Soldiers," I replied.

"You're right, but that's not why I'm here," she said in a stronger and more confident voice—not yet commensurate to her rank, however. "The problem goes way back. I left home at the age of seventeen, as soon as I could. My mother tormented me, and her boyfriends had their way with me. She never believed me when I told her that they'd crawl into my bed at night." Wendy untangled her legs and stretched them out in front of her, toes pointed. "I went to therapy for that already. You don't have to worry about it; it's not why I'm here," she said again, shooing away the topic with her hand.

I nodded. "All these variables come into play, Wendy, but I hear what you mean. Please, continue." I clasped my hands together.

"I felt guilty when I enlisted because I left my kid brother, Evan, behind. He was like my son. I raised him because our mother was never home. I was five when Evan was born. He was my baby doll. I cooked and cleaned for him, wiped his ass, potty trained him, disciplined him, tutored him, put him into bed, you name it—I did it for him. We were each other's world—all we ever had." She bit her lip so hard the skin cracked and bled bright-red over the white tissue she held. She watched the droplet of blood expand throughout the soft fibers.

"Mom treated Evan better. She didn't beat him, like she beat me. My last shrink said my mom saw herself in me, hated herself, and therefore hated me. I can see that. It makes all too much sense." She tossed the blanket off her lap, irritated by her thoughts. "Every day I was told I was a piece of sh** who would never amount to anything. So I kidnapped Evan in an attempt to escape, but that ended in a disaster. I told CPS about the abuse we experienced in our home, but they just gave me the middle finger when my mom showed up to sweet-talk them in her frilly pink apron and her fake-as-sh** Southern drawl. She told them I had mental issues, and they believed her. No one gave a sh** about us kids. I tried, Ma'am." Wendy looked at me for approval. "I didn't stop trying to rescue, Evan. I swear it."

"I believe you, Wendy," I replied.

"Finally, I decided it was enough, so I marched my seventeen-year-old self to the Army recruiter and said, 'How early can you get me the hell outta here?' Three days later, on my birthday, I sat my happy ass on the bus to MEPS and then Basic Training. It was the second-best birthday present I ever received. I only had one before it—a bouquet of flowers with soil dangling from the roots, picked right from the neighbors' garden—a gift from Evan when he was about seven."

"That was a courageous decision, Wendy."

"I only did it because I believed that Evan would be okay." She shrugged her shoulders. "Mom didn't pull crazy stunts on Evan; she saved those for me." She shook her head with emphasis. "At thirteen, Evan was old enough to defend himself. Plus, he had my phone number. He knew I'd drop everything for him if he needed me—at least, I thought he knew that." Wendy seemed to try and convince herself.

"I visited Evan every Christmas. I saved up to take him to a ski resort each year—nothing too fancy." She whimpered. "But Evan wasn't the same by the time he was seventeen. He was hostile and into drugs, hanging with the wrong crowds. He didn't listen to me." Wendy's bottom lip began to bleed again, but she didn't notice.

"Our last Christmas at the resort was 2007. We fought the entire drive there. Evan seemed high on some sh**. He wasn't himself. He yelled and cursed at me for abandoning him. Evan blamed me for his sh**ty life." Wendy retreated back to her canopy of red hair and tears poured down her cheeks. "He couldn't see past his pain. I wanted to f***ing strangle him." She gestured the motion with both her hands in the air.

"I don't think any amount of insight you gave him would've mattered at that time," I replied.

"Evan disappeared into the bathroom for hours that night. I pleaded for him to come out, but he refused. Finally, I fell asleep and woke up two hours later. I gently knocked on the bathroom door and he responded with 'Just go to sleep.'" Wendy crossed her arms and began bobbing her legs. "I should've just forced myself in on him, but I respected his request." She wrapped her arms around her body in an almost strangling hug. "I didn't go back to bed. I was too distraught.

So instead, I walked into the snow-covered woods to settle my mind. But I shouldn't have left."

She took a deep breath and spoke in an audible whisper. "When I returned to our room, Evan was laying on the bed, passed out. My heart melted, seeing him peaceful and finally out of the damn bathroom. I knew that once he slept it off, we'd be back into our brother-sister groove."

Her tears continued to flow. "I knew it would all be okay, so I took my sweet time peeling off the layers of my winter clothes. I wrapped myself in the complimentary bathrobe and tiptoed to Evan's bedside. I ran my fingers through his thick blond hair, the way I soothed him when he was a child." She inhaled several fluttered breaths. "I was so caught up in that peaceful moment that it took me a minute to realize he wasn't breathing."

She flattened a stack of tissues and buried her face in it. She looked up at me and in one quick breath said, "I flipped him over on the bed and searched for a pulse, but there was nothing." Bursts of tears dripped from her chin onto her black shirt. "I guided his body to the floor, using the quilt. I did chest compressions for what felt like eternity." Wendy straightened her arms in the shape of a V, her clasped hands together, as she subconsciously imitated the motion. When she noticed her position, she instantly released her arms, and her fingers found her hair once more.

"I only left his side to call 911." Wendy inhaled forcefully. "I sat with his head in my lap, and I watched my tears fall and roll down his pale white cheeks; I cried for the both of us." She dropped her hands and caressed the white flower tattoo with her fingers. "I sang Evan his favorite lullaby—'Edelweiss.' I sang it over and over again through every convulsing sob."

My eyes welled up with tears.

Wendy's eyes widened, and she took in a deep breath, shifting the energy in the room. She pointed to herself and said, *"Evan f***ing abandoned me!"* She pronounced every syllable.

She grabbed her shoes and put them on. She pulled up her socks, emphasizing the intentional covering of her edelweiss tattoo. "The next day, Doc"—Wendy bit her lip—"the recruiter called me to confirm Evan's enlistment appointment."

Wendy perceived herself to be a chronic "abandoner" after the death of her brother. She believed that every negative life experience since his death was the result of her abandoning others, just as she was abandoned as a child. She worked through nearly a dozen sessions of Rhythm Restoration with tremendous success. She needed to emotionally digest her painful childhood before confronting her greatest hurt. It took several sessions for her to forgive her mother and surrender her hurt, pain, and suffering to God. Wendy learned that she didn't have to reconcile the relationship with her mother in order to grant forgiveness. Her mother planted toxic seeds in her mind that grew into deep-rooted poison: shame and a sense of being unlovable and unworthy. Wendy finally decided to rip that poison out and replace it with God's love. In the process, she set herself free from the captivity of resenting her mother. Forgiveness served foremost to set Wendy free.

☆ ☆ ☆

Session 5

"SPC Conner Conway was nineteen years old," Wendy said as she stared off into the distance. Today she sat in the middle of the sofa, wearing her camouflage battle uniform with her hair slicked back in a low, perfectly twisted bun.

"Tell me more about Conway," I asked her.

It was imperative for her to recognize Conway's life in order to replace the image of his death so deeply burned into her mind.

Wendy simply closed her eyes and sat completely still. "If my brother had lived to join the Army, Conway would've been his all-around doppelganger," she replied. One glistening tear rolled down her cheek. "SPC Conway had dirty-blond hair and aqua eyes, just like Evan; it was truly remarkable." She shook her head quickly as if the image in her mind was an Etch A Sketch and she wanted it gone. "I can only remember his face in his last moments." She searched my eyes for answers.

"That's not uncommon, Wendy." I asked, "Do you want to try Rhythm Restoration on that? It helped you find closure with Evan and your mother."

"Sure," she sighed. "I have nothing to lose at this point."

"All right, I want you to bring your favorite memories of Conway to mind." It was imperative for her to recognize Conway's life in order to replace the image of his death so deeply burned into her mind.

<Rhythm Restoration>

"What did you experience?" I asked.

"The first time Conway reported to my office was for failure to report to morning formation. I swear that knucklehead f***ed up the reporting protocol at least half a dozen times." She laughed and a genuine smile spread across her face; it was contagious. This was the first time I noticed the small gap between her two front teeth. "I broke my bearing and laughed so hard, and then he laughed, and then I had to smoke the sh** out of him [push-ups] for breaking his bearing. He never missed a formation after that—never. Conway always tried so hard to prove himself to me," she said, her fingers fumbling for the pressed seams in her uniform.

"It's nice to see you smile, Wendy. Let's continue to bring back those positive memories and press onward," I said.

<Rhythm Restoration>

"What did you experience?" I asked.

"I remember how big his smile was when he saw me walk into chapel for the first time. I took him up on his invitation when my Xbox broke." She laughed. "I never missed a service after that. Conway was the reason I found God. I had a terrible mother and an absent father, so I deserved a heavenly one who'd love me unconditionally and never abandon me. I found God in the midst of war." She swallowed hard, as if choking down a jagged pill. "I owe my salvation to Conway."

"Conway was your second chance in more ways than one, Wendy. First and foremost, he directed you to Jesus. And then you had the opportunity to have a second chance with a boy just like your brother," I explained. "It's time now to confront that day ..."

She nodded and courageously began tapping before I could even prompt her. Her tears were reflexive, and her rhythm was painful—slow and forced.

<Rhythm Restoration>

"What did you experience?" I asked.

"His confusion. His fear. The terror in his eyes when I found him."
She brought her legs onto the sofa and hugged them, gently rocking
herself from side to side. "I don't think I even told you the full story,"
she said. I shook my head. "I was so impressed by SPC Conway's performance during one of our last convoys. He maneuvered the vehicles
with perfection, guiding the drivers out of an IED choke hold. He used
the radio like a pro—relaying information back and forth to the tactical
operations center." She stopped rocking. "1SGT and I thought it was
time for him to be the driver in the lead vehicle during our next mission.
He'd proven himself, and he deserved that leadership promotion." She
shook her head and furrowed her brows. "We made sure he had all the
support he needed. In fact, I rode in the rear of the lead vehicle, which
he was driving—a dozen vehicles in the convoy. 1SGT rode in the last
vehicle."

She pulled five tissues slowly from the box, stimulating her
fingertips with the soft fibers. "SPC Conway was stoked about the
opportunity." She blotted her eyes. "Before we rolled out at zero dark
thirty, he confirmed a checklist with me inside the lit vehicle. He was,
'Yes, Ma'am, this-and-that.' Conway was on point. I knew it was the
right decision. We did our head count and rolled out."

Wendy searched my eyes for grounding, focused on me, and took
deep breaths. I held her gaze, as I was her anchor in that moment.

"The TOC came on the radio, informing us of suspicious activity
on the route we chose. It was the longer of the two routes, but we knew
it like the back of our hands. Our other option was the short route that
we had only navigated once before, but it was high traffic." She drew in
a deep breath like taking a drag from one of her Virginia Slims. "It was
a toss-up, so I let SPC Conway decide. He chose the short route, feeling
confident that he remembered the layout of the land. I agreed, giving

him the illusion that he had more autonomy than he really did. I wish I had never done that." She ignored her tears and kept on.

"It was still dark out. We fell into the rumbling comfort of the humming, up-armored beasts that rolled beneath us." She paused. "And then time froze," she whispered. Her fingers traced the sides of her face until they found her ears and protectively covered them. "The sound of the explosion left a high-pitch buzz ringing in our ears. We looked frantically at one another, patting down our bodies to make sure we were still intact. I turned to my right and left to make sure my Soldiers were okay. The impact rang the sh** out of our bells, but we had to be on point—this was life or death." She looked around the room for another distraction, she wanted so badly to escape this memory.

"Stay with it, Wendy," I said as I handed her the blanket that hung neatly folded on the back of my chair. She welcomed the soft texture and pulled it over her legs.

"I pushed myself into the front seat to check on Conway. His body was slumped over the steering wheel. My heart stopped when I saw that." She wiped her face with her bare hands. "His chest expanded, so I rattled his body hard and screamed his name into his bleeding ear until he was conscious." She swallowed hard. "Conway looked at me and gave me a thumbs-up and a crooked smile. Everyone was accounted for in our vehicle. I yanked the radio out of his hand and called for a head count of all the vehicles. 'Vehicle two, all accounted for?' Radio silence. 'Yes, Major.' 'Vehicle three, all accounted for?' Radio silence. More radio silence. F***. It was time for recovery."

"I jumped out of the vehicle first." Both of Wendy's combat boots plopped to the floor from the sofa as she found herself completely engaged in the memory. "The high-pitched tone still rang in my ears, and the potent smell of burning tires filled my nostrils." She coughed as if the same smell was affecting her in the present moment.

"I was high on adrenaline, and nothing was going to get in my way. Vehicle three was in flames. The back seat looked as if a blender had spun through it—two passengers were undoubtedly dead. I went straight for the Soldier who hung halfway out of the vehicle; both his legs were like strands of spaghetti. There was so much blood covering his face, I didn't know who he was." She wiped her face in a circular motion with both hands, as if to clean it. "I quickly found a pulse and screamed for help. *'Where's the medic?'* A voice from underneath mumbled, 'That's me.'" She stomped her foot on the floor and said, "'F***. It's SGT Gates, my medic.'" She removed her hair tie and placed it around her wrist. "'I got you, SGT. You're going to be okay,' I said.

"Conway ran to my aid. He scoured the back seat of the vehicle searching for the medical supplies." Wendy grabbed her chest and swallowed hard to keep her nausea at bay. "Conway ran out with the first aid kit. He pulled out the tourniquets and, with perfect technique, wound them tightly around what remained of SGT's legs while I poured the coagulant all over his exposed flesh." Wendy began dry coughing and clearing her throat, then stood up to suck in the cold air that poured out from the vents. Then she closed her eyes to let the frigid air strike her face and dry her tears.

"My team pulled out the driver, while Conway and I worked on SGT Gates. But the driver was gone." She sat down and grabbed hold of the back of her neck with her right hand. "SGT Gates looked at Conway through the mask of blood and said, 'Don't let me die.' Conway replied, 'You're safe, brother. Nothing is going to happen to you, I promise.'" Wendy began to hyperventilate. She stood up and paced the room, back and forth like a caged animal. She unbuttoned her ACU blouse, ripped herself out of it, and tossed it on the sofa.

I said, "Wendy, engage your combat breathing; find something to focus on."

She nodded, focused intently out the window at the rapidly shifting clouds, and placed her hand across her chest to monitor her breathing. "We laid SGT Gates on the floor of our vehicle. It was bizarre to see how he fit perfectly without his legs. I took over the driver's seat and navigated us back to the CSH (combat support hospital). Conway sat behind my seat, holding SGT Gates's hand. He wiped the blood off his face with medical wipes and sat staring at him. 'Conway, keep your focus on me,' I shouted at him through the rearview mirror. I looked up every now and again to make sure his eyes were still tethered to me, and he stared at me the entire hour.

"We delivered SGT Gates to the CSH. With all the chaos in the operating room, Conway was able to linger in the background. I sat outside the tent, just close enough to hear what was happening. The high-pitched buzzing in my head returned, but it didn't drown out the sound of SGT Gate's flatline. We lost him too. Four in one day. I didn't cry then—I couldn't. They all looked to me for strength." She stared at me pensively. "You know what it's like. You have to be ten times stronger as a woman commander. There's no room for weakness or else they'll eat you alive."

"Yes, Wendy," I replied.

"Conway sprinted out of the CSH, and I let him go. When I break down, I need my space, so I respected his. The next day, I caught Conway staring at the exploded Humvee as it was being washed in the maintenance bay. He seemed hypnotized by the blood that collected at the drain before it swirled into the sewage." Wendy began pulling and snapping her hair tie against her wrist. "I grabbed Conway by the arm and led him away from there." She pulled and snapped the hair tie again. "'You need to stop that, Conway. It wasn't your fault. Not the least bit. You did everything you could do. We cannot control these things. I'm proud of how quickly and diligently you executed yesterday, but we don't win all the battles. When you're ready to talk, I'm here, lil' brother.' He just looked at me and shook his head. I waited for him to respond, but he said nothing. Then he slapped his heels together and asked, 'Permission to be excused, Ma'am?' 'Yes,' I replied. He didn't listen to me," Wendy said, her breathing stifled.

"Later, I stood in the corner of the DFAC searching for Conway, but he wasn't there. I felt it in my gut." Wendy wrapped her arms around her stomach and leaned forward. "Something wasn't right. So I ran to his bunk. I swung the door open." She made a white-knuckled fist. "And there he was"—her voice caught in her throat—"sitting across the room on his bed with his M9 in his mouth." She smashed her fist into the sofa. "He stared at me, but he never dropped his weapon. I thought he would, but he didn't, so I lunged for him as he pulled the f***ing trigger." She collapsed and sat crying for several racing heartbeats.

"Breathe, Wendy," I said.

She finally looked up and she spoke in a hushed voice. "His body slumped onto the bed. Bright-red blood sprayed the wall behind him. I ran to him and took his face in my hands." Wendy imitated her clasped hands around his face. "In just seconds, I watched him turn from flush to white. His beautiful aqua eyes turned gray, so I gently closed them. I watched my tears fall from my face onto his cheeks. It was the second time that I cried for the both of us."

☆ ☆ ☆

"I don't remember much of what happened after that. It was a blur of people rushing in and out of the room." She paused and grabbed her upper arm. "I remember the grip of being ripped from his side by two MPs. I was f***ing handcuffed and taken in for questioning." She looked up at me. "Can you believe that?"

"Not at all," I replied.

"Apparently it was suspicious that I was lying with his dead body, singing that lullaby I sang to Evan, 'Edelweiss.' I don't remember any of it." She shook her head. "Hours later they released me—no apology. It felt like I'd sat there for eternity, drenched in Conway's blood." She stood up briefly to tug at her uniform. "I stood in the shower for hours, watching his blood swirl down the drain." She zoned out, and when she came back, she looked at me and said, "I blame myself for his death."

"Why?" I asked.

"Because I abandoned him like I did my brother. If I'd been more present for him, he'd still be alive," Wendy replied as if it was an obvious fact.

There is absolutely no guarantee that if you had intervened more strongly, they would still be alive.

"Help me understand how you abandoned Conway and Evan," I said gently. "You've taken responsibility for something you had no control over. You may feel as though you had some *influence*, but you did not have *control*."

"Exactly, my influence could've saved their lives. It's my fault I didn't intervene more strongly."

"Wendy, there is absolutely no guarantee that if you had intervened more strongly, they would still be alive." She took in a deep breath. "So why didn't you intervene more strongly, Wendy?" I asked. I knew I was being abrasive, but it was with good intent.

She paused and her eyes searched the room as her brain pieced together the answer. "Because, I hate it when people do that to me. I need to get over things in my own time. I hate being emotionally bombarded by others when I'm trying to make sense of something myself."

"Exactly. I see how you are in session. You take time to examine your thoughts before releasing them to the world. You respected Evan and Conway in the same way—treating them the way you'd want to be treated."

She nodded.

"If I'm not mistaken, you spoke to both of them just before their deaths. You let them know you were there, you gave your words of wisdom, and you let them decide what to do with them." I counted on each of my fingers so she could physically see the amount of effort she had made. "How is that abandonment?"

"It doesn't seem like it. But it feels like I've abandoned every relationship, like with my mother, my brother, and now Conway."

"It sounded more like your mother abandoned you first, and then you learned to live a life without her when you took over her parental responsibilities, right?"

"Yes. I didn't think of it quite like that."

"And your brother. You came back every year for Evan and paved a future for him. Is that abandonment?"

"No."

"Now, Conway. You already figured that one out. You were giving him space to process and you let him know you were available when he needed you."

Wendy nodded and said, "You can lead a horse to water, but you can't force it to drink—even when it's dehydrated and dying."

"Yes. Wendy, I truly believe that if you could've changed the outcome, you would've—to the point of sacrificing your own life for theirs," I said.

"Without a doubt," Wendy replied.

"Does the collection of your responses sound like abandonment?" I asked in a serious tone.

"No."

Outside, the cloud formations shifted and sunlight poured into the office. Wendy looked out, squinting her eyes. She sat deep in thought for several moments. "Did Conway make it to heaven?" she asked. "You know what some people believe about those who choose to take their own lives …"

I was completely caught off guard, so I silently asked God for help. I opened my desk drawer and pulled out a small book of Scriptures. "I'm certain Conway is at peace in the presence of God." I looked at Wendy, sitting perched on the edge of her seat. "Nowhere in the Bible does it say that suicide is an unforgivable sin. How many times do people die after sinning and fail to ask for forgiveness? I'm sure far more than those who have the opportunity to do so. We serve a loving and merciful God who demonstrates His affection for us through acts of grace." Tears formed in Wendy's eyes. "'For I am convinced that neither death nor life, neither angels nor demons, neither the present nor the future, nor any powers, neither height nor depth, nor anything else in all creation, will be able to separate us from the love of God that is in Christ Jesus our Lord.' That's in Romans 8:38–39."

"Thank you," Wendy whispered.

☆ ☆ ☆

Wendy was finally able to replace the memory of Conway's lifeless face with the image of his bright-eyed smile. In fact, she drew a beautiful portrait of him and mustered up the courage to mail it to his mother, Shirley, in Nashville. She enclosed a letter addressing how she felt about Conway with her drawing. On a handmade card, decorated in cloth flowers and taped to a tin of homemade red-velvet cookies, Shirley responded in perfect cursive:

Honey, the picture you drew brought tremendous joy to my heart. You captured Conner's spirit in his eyes and his smile. I would do anything to see that brought to life again. Conner respected your leadership and wanted to grow up to be an officer like you. I thank you for how you inspired him.

You wrote about how you wished you could have saved him. Baby, that wasn't for you to do; you could not control that. Conner was deeply hurt and did something out of tremendous fear. It wasn't the Conner we knew and loved who pulled the trigger that day. He was in the clutches of the Enemy, but now he is free. Honey, I want you to stop blaming yourself from this moment on. We take away from Conner's peace when we blame ourselves for his death. Let's all make peace, together. Conner is with God, baby. We will all see him again, I promise.

Wendy's circle of love only continued to grow—a reflection of God's love for her and her willingness to follow His lead.

Session 7

"Wendy, I want you to visualize how God sees you. Perhaps visualize yourself approaching Him and simply asking, 'Lord, how do You see me?' Do you think you can do that?"

<Rhythm Restoration>

Wendy opened her eyes less than twenty seconds later. She shook her head in disbelief. "I visualized approaching Jesus. His face was so perfect and His expression so sincere." A tear rolled down her cheek. "Jesus said, 'When I see you, I see Me.'"

I was amazed at Wendy's progress. "Throughout the Bible, there are many verses about how we wear a crown as part of God's royal family. It speaks about how we will receive the crown of life if we remain steadfast during times of tribulation. After everything you've been through, I want you to visualize your coronation ceremony with your heavenly Father."

Tears rolled down Wendy's pink cheeks and she began visualizing again.

<Rhythm Restoration>

Silently, I prayed for God to inspire Wendy with a vision to promote her healing. It's always incredible to watch God show up in this process. "What did you experience?" I asked.

For several heartbeats, Wendy simply stared out the window at the deep-blue sky. "Well, don't laugh ..." A bright smile suddenly parted the clouds of her sullen expression. "It's so cheesy—like a scene in some teenybopper princess movie."

She laughed. "Well, I walked down a long golden carpet as I approached the throne where Jesus stood with my crown. On the right side of Jesus was Evan and on the left was Conway." Her faucet of tears turned on in an instant. "Evan approached me before I could reach the throne. He wrapped his arms around me so tight and spoke. He said, 'Thank you for loving me unconditionally. It was the closest to the love of our Lord that I had ever received. You never left me—just as Jesus never left me. I'm sorry for the hurtful words I said. I was under the influence of some terrible things. Wendy, I want you to know this: I didn't kill myself that night. I died of an overdose. But look at me now: I'm okay." Wendy covered her mouth with her hand and gasped. "Then he kissed my cheek and tucked a perfect edelweiss behind my ear. He's watching over me." Wendy touched her head where she imagined the flower to sit.

"Please, tell me more," I said.

"Well, I continued to walk to the throne, and then Conway approached me. He said, 'I'm sorry, Wendy. It wasn't me who pulled that trigger. I had lost myself in that moment; I was filled with shame and fear. It wasn't your fault, Ma'am. I made the choice. Your brother is right. Your love is like His.' Conway looked at Jesus, who smiled softly at us both. I was speechless as I squeezed the eternal life out of him." Wendy laughed at her cheesy joke, and I joined in. "I told Conway 'Thank you for leading me to Jesus and, quite literally, saving my life.' Then he placed another edelweiss behind my other ear.

"I walked to the throne, and Jesus said, 'See? They see you the way I see you. Your hurt and suffering is never a waste. Trust Me, I know what it's like, My daughter.' He showed me the scars on His wrists. 'Now, look at us; see where we are now.' He took a moment to show me a glimpse of heaven, and then He touched the two flowers the boys had given me before placing a crown of wildflowers on my head."

Wendy closed her eyes. "It was a waterfall of flowers dripping from my crown and woven into my hair—so many vibrant colors that the two edelweiss stood out, pure and white."

It was amazing to see God's work in Wendy's life—a true testament to Romans 8:28: "And we know that God causes all things to work together for good to those who love God, to those who are called according to His purpose" (NASB).

Part III

Miracles in Combat

*God's proximity on the battlefield and
how He makes beauty from ashes*

Chapter 10

MIRACLE ON THE BATTLEFIELD

SPC Corbin (Army) is a fictional character whose emotional experiences accurately reflect those of many combat veterans. Told in a first-person account, this is his story.

The decayed flesh reeks. It's not a smell I can get used to. The wild animals will come for it. And when they do, we'll have no choice but to fire shots, exposing our cover. We're already low on ammunition as it is.

SPC Kilbourn hasn't stopped crying since we got blasted twenty-four hours ago. He's squatting in the corner of the ravine with his head buried in his folded arms. "Dude, Kilbourn! Shut up already!" I yell at him. He sucks in a deep, quivering breath and flips me off. "We have one gallon of water left for the four of us, and your dumba** is wasting it on tears. Look at you … your face is disgusting."

"F*** off, man!" he replies as his filthy hands smear dirt and tears across his flushed face.

"Be productive. Check Lee's pulse," I command as I point to the ground where a Soldier lies curled up on a litter. I'd do it, but I'm busy accounting for all the resources we've managed to salvage since the blast.

SPC Kilbourn swallows hard, sits up straight, and crawls toward SPC Lee. Carefully, he takes Lee's wrist and swallows again to be still enough to detect his pulse. "He's still alive, but his pulse is weak," announces Kilbourn.

SGT Moran is busy trying to get the coms (communications) to work. The blast percussion damaged them. After parceling out our goods to sustain us for the next forty-eight hours, I kneel beside Lee. It's time to swap out the tourniquet on his shrapnel wound and place it higher up his leg. Nothing will keep the maggots off his dangling, decayed flesh.

I can't do this without switching my mindset, so I close my eyes until I'm back on the farm during hunting season. I imagine it's time to skin a deer. I inhale the metallic scent of blood and exhale fear. Using my Ka-Bar, I do what I must.

Kilbourn heaves, one hand cupping his mouth and the other hugging his stomach. In a split second, he hops outta the ravine and vomits his MRE. What a waste of calories! God knows how long we'll be stuck here.

"Idiot! Get back here," SGT yells.

The first shots pop off. Kilbourn dives back into the ravine. F***ing dumba** blew our cover. I pull the blood-saturated tourniquet tight until my knuckles turn white. Hastily, I wipe my bloody hands down the side of my uniform and search for my weapon.

"Take cover and fire!" shouts SGT.

"Roger," I quickly respond.

Suddenly, Kilbourn activates his alter ego, RoboCop. He retrieves his weapon and tosses me mine. It lands in my palm with magnetic force. WTF happened to him? "Kilbourn" just transformed into "*bourn to kil.*" It's about damn time! In sync, we fall in beside SGT Moran and engage the enemy.

In the pink haze of sunset, the bullets ricochet off the ground in bright-orange bursts. They're coming in hot—faster and with more force. We gotta be outnumbered at least three to one.

"SPC Corbin, account for our ammo," shouts SGT Moran.

"SGT, only enough to last us for another five minutes at this rate."

"God help us," he replies, unflinching.

I return to my weapon and silently repeat his words over and over again. *God help us. God help us. God help us.* My heart ricochets in my chest like the bullets popping off the ground. I force the words out of my mouth: "SGT, what do you want us to do when we run out?"

"Game over," he stoically replies. "Return fire, SPC.… So help me God, if we're going down, we're going down with a bang."

Now I know how I'm going to die. How do I confront my own death behind a magazine cartridge? Only nineteen years old … so many things I didn't get to do. My pity party catches momentum and begins to spiral out of control. I suppose it's better me than some guy with a family like SGT. *Sh**.* Some may say that dying in combat is a glorious way to go. They'll call me a hero. *Hero.* The word doesn't sit well.

But what if the enemy captures me? My body heat rises at the thought of a bag over my head and a knife at my throat. Will they start sawing my head off while I'm still alive? Or will they show mercy and slice my throat first? My fear boils over into a cowardly question that involuntarily rushes from my lips: "SGT, should we save enough ammo to kill ourselves before they take us hostage?"

"You're not a coward, SPC. Get your f***ing head in the game. It's not over till it's over, kid."

I don't understand how he's so calm and collected right now. "Grace under f***ing fire" is the only way to describe him.

I'm not a coward. I speak aloud, "God, help me. Help us, Lord. We have won this battle." Confidence floods me, and my voice becomes stronger, "In the name of Jesus, we are free from this enemy. We are not their prisoners. In the name of Jesus, we are victorious … In the name of Jesus, *we are* victorious …" Together, we declare these words in cadence as we stare off into the darkness interrupted by bursts of bright lights.

My mind slips back two years ago to my second visit to church. It was then that I decided to bring all my life's problems to the altar. Tearfully, I prayed to be liberated from the lifetime effects of child abuse. It was a miracle that I survived my father's drunken episodes. He hated me, so I hated me. I prayed for love and healing for my broken self.

I walked outta the church only to be stopped as soon as I stepped out the door. This man put his hand gently on my shoulder, and I was surprised I didn't flinch. He was intimidating in his crisp uniform: his service dress. He had butterscotch skin and pale green eyes that reflected the goodness of God. It sounds so stupid, I know, but it's true. I swear.

"Let me pray for you, son …" His words filled every void and broken part of me. *Son.* No one ever called me by that word in a sober state or without clenched fists. To hear that word drop softly from his lips to my heart disarmed me, as if God had spoken through him. He reinvented that word for me.

"Son, He who is in you is greater than he who is in the world. There is nothing you can do that will separate you from our heavenly Father, but you have to want Him. You need to know that He wants you, more than you could possibly believe." That man was the closest thing to Christ I have ever encountered. It was a simple prayer and that was all, no exchange of contact information. He just went on with his blessed life, and I was changed forever. How?

There is nothing you can do that will separate you from our heavenly Father.... You need to know that He wants you.

I wanted to be like him. Twenty-four hours later, we were face to face again, but this time not at church. The look of shock on our faces was priceless. He was a recruiter. It was God's will, clear as day, and here I am—where I'm meant to be. *Where I'm meant to be.* An incredible peace comes over me. *Where I'm meant to be. Nothing can separate Him from me: not this situation, not death. No matter what, I will be okay. I'm okay.*

The sweat stops invading my vision. I reload my weapon without having to wipe my brow. This is it—my last magazine. There will be no more bullets left to reload once I run out.

I continue to engage the enemy—shoulder to shoulder with the honorable men I will die beside. Throughout my life, I've never felt like I've belonged until now.... Even in the midst of combat ... I belong to them—my brothers. *Thank You, God.* I never thought I'd feel this way. I love my brothers. That sounds so f***ing cheesy. But this feeling is a miracle for someone like me. If I must die, I'll die holding on to this feeling of love. Where there is love, there is God. He's here right now.

Who would've guessed that the deepest thought process of my life would take place behind the barrel of an M4 carbine? This was supposed to happen in my golden years rocking in a chair on my front porch.

I reel my brain back to the firefight. The darkness sets in, blacking out our targets in an uncertain twilight. Our lives will set with that sun.

Damn it, I'm out of ammunition. Moran and Kilbourn are still going at it, but that will only last for a minute or so. I crawl to check on Lee. There's nothing I can do for him but pray. I'd rather focus on him than me in the last moments of my life. It's truly a blessing that he's unconscious right now.

The bullets ricochet inches above my head. I could just stand up and it would all be over in an instant—no worry about what would happen next.

"What the f*** now? I'm out," shouts SPC Kilbourn.

"Take anything that can be used as a weapon. Resist and evade." The words quickly fall from SGT's lips, almost slurred.

My heart beats in my ears like an amplified drum. Not knowing what to expect is terrifying. I remind myself, *Greater is He who is in me than he who is in the world.*

"What about Lee?" I ask as I crawl toward SGT.

"No man left behind. He's mine!" SGT replies, breathless. Hope drains from his eyes as he looks down at Lee's limp body: deadweight. They won't get far.

My heart crashes to the pit of my knotted stomach. They don't deserve that. "No—I got him. You have a family, SGT. He's mine."

SGT shakes his head in defiance and discretely wipes the tears from his eyes.

"What the f*** is happening? Are you guys for real?" SPC Kilbourn turns his back to the enemy and looks directly at me. His watery blue eyes catch mine for just a heartbeat.

And then the most unbelievable thing happens in the distance! I see 'em in the middle of the combat zone.

"What the f***!" I reply. Kilbourn's head swivels around to see what I see. "Sh**, that was fast. They're here for us!" shouts Kilbourn in a state of panic.

"I dunno," I reply, and the firefight abruptly stops.

"It's our own!" exclaims SGT.

The silhouettes appear to be a company of Soldiers about two clicks out: Special Forces, maybe? They outnumber the enemy two to one, at the very least. Everything is silent. It's as if they just materialized in the darkness, and now they're approaching the enemy.

"What do we do?" I ask.

"Stay put, and check on Lee," SGT replies with a new energy. He cracks a ChemLight before everything goes pitch black. The soft green glow is enough to light up the ravine.

As soon as I reach for Lee, the radio crackles—*signal!* I whip around. SGT stares wide-eyed in disbelief at the lit-up radio in his hand. "Oh my God—it's a miracle," he says.

Lee takes a labored breath in and out, yet mine is filled with hope. If he only knew that this just might work out for all of us. "We need a bird; he doesn't have much time!" I shout.

"Thirty minutes," SGT replies.

We got this. "We got this," I whisper to Lee as I brush back his matted jet-black hair and clean his face with a wet bandage. "We got this, brother ... I'm here. I'm not going anywhere. We got this ..." Tears stream from my eyes, and I break my bearing.

"Lock it up, son!" SGT places his hand on my shoulder.

Son. There it is again—that word. The new meaning of it disarms me. I swallow the hard lump in my throat. Kilbourn, SGT, and I kneel facing one another.

SPC Kilbourn looks back at the horizon and says, "They disappeared as quickly as they arrived."

"Should we investigate?" I ask, looking into SGT's black eyes.

"No," SPC Kilbourn interrupts, answering on SGT's behalf.

"Stand by," SGT replies and then speaks into the crackling radio: "The company that just diverted the TIC (troops in contact), who were they?"

"SGT, the bird is coming. We will send QRF (quick reaction force) alongside it. No teams in contact now or ever at that location. They're on their way. Stand by, SGT," replies the voice over the radio.

"That squad was nobody?" I ask. We stare at one another in the green illumination, completely dumfounded. "They were just a vision? A vision shared by all of us—even the enemy who backed down because of it?" I ask.

SGT looks down at his radio. "This had no connectivity." He shakes his head. "What the f***? Have we all lost our minds?" he asks, looking at both of us intently.

SPC Kilbourn can't get the words out fast enough: "F***, no. That was a miracle. A legit miracle!"

In unison we inhale deeply, but we don't exhale, because as soon as we do, sh** will go boom. It's not time to let our guard down—not yet.

A thundering sound breaks through the night. We drop to the ground and reach for our weapons. I'm hovering over Lee's body.

"It's just the bird," yells SGT above the noise of the thudding propellers that create a sand-whipping vortex in the ravine.

The sound of shouting pararescue jumpers sets us free from the captivity of unshakeable fear.

"Body count?" shouts one of the PJs.

"One man down—still alive," I reply and step aside to allow him to take Lee away.

"Stay low to the ground," another PJ shouts.

"Our belongings?" I ask.

"We got it. Board the bird. Now move!" he yells as he adjusts his night vision goggles.

I crawl out of the ravine and get tossed into the bird by someone I can't see. It's complete blackout; I can't see my hands just one inch in front of me.

Once loaded and prepped for takeoff, I allow myself to finally exhale. It was never my breath to hold on to.... It was, and will always be, His. I'd rather have it that way ... with Him in control. I'm useless without Him. *Thank You, Jesus!* Today, our lives didn't set with the sun—only our fears and disbelief went down with it.

I pull the straps of my seatbelt too tight—any tighter would cut off my blood flow. I attempt to muster my energy to brace for the worst-case scenario—crash and burn. But I have no energy. At this point, it is what it is. I've made peace with my life and death in Christ. He's the realest thing I know.

☆ ☆ ☆

When will I run out of miracles? Are they like wishes? I know that idea is stupid and untrue, but it prompts me to reflect on all the possible miracles I've taken for granted—like watching Kilbourn, of all people, accept Jesus. I can't see him, but I hear him praying, even above the whipping sound of the propellers. You'll never find an atheist in a foxhole. I swallow a small laugh.

I close my eyes as images pass through my mind like scenery through the window of a train. I fed a village of starving families and played soccer with local children. I made friendships with my interpreters, though guarded. I saw my brothers- and sisters-in-arms discover a sense of family and support among each other. Perhaps laughter, love, compassion, and peace between perceived enemies are miracles too … miracles on the battlefield.

I reach down to touch Lee, who lies on the stretcher at my feet. I fumble for his arm, but I can't distinguish his pulse on the choppy flight. I pray for his life and thank God for how He saved mine. As the bird descends, I mentally rehearse my next steps upon landing.

But before I can even unbuckle myself from my seat, a waiting team floods the bird. Four medics evacuate Lee, place him in the back of a truck, and drive him off to the CSH. Another team of medics swarms me, but I break through their outstretched arms and run straight to find Lee.

The blood pulses through my head, and I hear a voice … loud and clear. *Remember the first miracle, son.* I shake my head in disbelief, but the phrase resonates three times—each time louder and clearer. *Remember the first miracle, son.*

I stumble past the sliding glass doors of the CSH and burst through the curtain dividers, asking, "Lee?" Each time I'm greeted with a deer-in-the-headlights look until finally someone says, "Operating room, but you can't go in there." *Watch me.* I run straight ahead, down the hall, and through the double doors. Footsteps follow at my heels. "Stop! Stop!" someone shouts.

Instantly I stop. All eyes are on me—expectant gazes awaiting my reaction. I follow their eyes to the center of the room, where Chaplain Paul is praying.

"He's gone," someone whispers as she gently touches my arm.

As I move closer to the operating table, the wall of blue scrubs parts. I reach for Lee's hand and slowly bring it close to my face. As I do, his paracord bracelet slips down his arm, revealing the tattoo of a small cross and the words "Prisoner of Hope."

Perhaps laughter, love, compassion, and peace between perceived enemies are miracles too.

Tears stream down my face. "You're not a prisoner anymore," I whisper. "You're free and blessed in the presence of our Savior. You lived well and saved so many lives in the midst of hell. God must be so pleased with you. I'll see you again, my brother."

Reflexively, the thought comes to mind: *With all these miracles, Lord, why couldn't You have just kept him alive? Why?*

And as I release my breath, it comes to me: *Remember the first miracle, son ...* My brain rewinds to my first experience, and then it hits me. It's not *my* first miracle; it's *the* first miracle. Our salvation, the promise of an eternal life in heaven with the Most High. And until then, we're blessed to live under His open heaven, receiving His undeserved, unmerited, and unearned grace and love—the abundant life. As Christ was a lamb whose blood was sacrificed for our salvation and everlasting life, so was Lee—a lamb whose blood was sacrificed for the freedom of our country, and my life.

As my fingers lightly graze his tattoo of the cross, I whisper, "I will always honor your sacrifice, my brother. Until I see you again."

Chapter 11

LAST WORDS LETTER

This fictional letter accurately reflects the events of many of our combat veterans when they lose loved ones.

My dearest daughter Callie,

You won't believe it, but your old man has been seeing a shrink. You're probably thinking, *It's about damn time.* Well, this doc instructed me to write a "last words" letter to you—a way to process that awful day, I suppose. I don't really know how to do this—forgive me for being all over the place—I was instructed to simply let it flow. I'm afraid that this may turn into a book but here goes nothing …

I'm glad you're not here to see who I've become since I lost you. I've been nothing but destructive. I'm trying to recover, my sweet girl. But some days, I feel it's impossible. I became a monster after your death. I cannot recognize who I've become. I don't deserve any good in my life—never.

I wasn't always the best father after my deployments. As you know—*knew* … damn, it kills me to refer to you in the past tense—I tried so hard to shield you from the awful things I saw in Iraq, with the hope that it wouldn't invade our relationship, like it had already invaded every other part of my mind. Sometimes I isolated myself from you because I didn't want to hurt you. You saw how painful it was when your best friend lost her father in war; he was my Soldier. I blamed myself for that. Sometimes I still believe it should've been me who died. You took such good care of your friend—she was the luckiest girl in the world to have you.

I'm sorry for avoiding you. I'm sorry I yelled and screamed. I'm sorry I was overly strict. And most of all, I'm sorry I didn't speak to you for a month after you chose to enlist. I hoped that my cold shoulder would deter you from the military life. But I should've known better. Once you had your mind set on something, nothing would stop you from achieving it. Right now I wish I could apologize to your blue eyes, warm flesh, and beating heart. I'm so sorry, Callie.

Sometimes I isolated myself from you because I didn't want to hurt you.

I have to let the paper dry before I write anymore. The ink won't stick where my tears have fallen.

I'm grateful I wasn't stupid enough to miss your Navy Corpsman graduation. You insisted that I wear my uniform to the commencement—the old Colonel Army guy with the beautiful Sailor. I had never been so proud until that day—our last hour together.

When I learned we'd deploy at the same time to Iraq, my heart became like a lion's—ferocious and protective. From a distance, I was determined to control all aspects of your life to keep you safe. You are … you were … you were my heart—the most precious aspect of my existence. I was vulnerable and terrified, knowing that my heart was beating outside of my chest. Thank you for putting up with my fears and understanding to the best of your ability why I was acting so crazy.

Now Father's Day is just around the corner. I can't breathe when I think about it. I blame that day—even though I know it's absolutely irrational ...

On Father's Day 2009, you were in Anbar Province and I was in Fallujah. I remember that day clearly. It all began around the firepit in the late afternoon. A couple of officers and I stood smoking the fine cigars your mother sent us to celebrate our special day. We bragged about our children and consoled each other about our chronic absence from their lives—justifying why it was necessary. We were enjoying our puffs until LT interrupted us to tell me about an urgent delivery.

I walked into our makeshift office space and was given a card with a gold Hallmark seal. In front of my desk was an oversized green duffle bag that looked to be filled with sandbags. I knew instantly that my goons were up to no good. I shook my head, rolled my eyes, and opened up the card, preparing for some stupid message. But I was wrong. It was a simple card from you, Callie. You wrote a beautiful message in it and placed a Polaroid pic of yourself inside. You were throwing a peace sign as you stood in front of the Camp Buehring monument. I stood and looked at that picture for too many moments, mesmerized by your smile and the light that radiated from your eyes. I could feel your energy in the mere presence of your pic.

As soon as I put the card down, LT summoned the Joes into the office. They filed in one at a time and created a large circle around me and the duffle bag. I shook my head knowing what was coming; they were gonna smoke me for Father's Day—little sh**bags.

LT opened the duffle and said, "I have a little Father's Day exercise for you." He reached in and pulled out a sandbag and threw it on the floor. I shook my head again; I knew where this was going. "I want you to"—as soon as he said that, *you* jumped out of the bag and LT finished his sentence—"hug your daughter." My heart pounded and I was sure this was a dream.

After feeling overwhelmed with joy, a tremendous fear rushed through me—the urgency to protect you. I used to have nightmares that I'd wake up on deployment to find my tiny daughter in the same godforsaken land as me. I'd have to abandon my mission to protect you. As panic filled my lungs, I locked up my emotion.

Everyone cheered. In Camp Fallujah, it was a rarity to witness so much excitement and happiness in one place.

Your mother was always so thoughtful about the items she sent in her care packages. She had a full-blown steak meal shipped to us that day. How she did it was beyond me. She even managed to coordinate this moment with our head cook, who prepared the meal in the most meticulous manner. Callie, we sat together in my office and had a daddy-daughter date by candlelight. I was the luckiest Soldier on deployment.

Your energy hit me like a tidal wave. I sat across from you, drenched in your excitement as you rattled on about your career. You saved so many lives; I couldn't be prouder. But I was afraid you'd experience that moment … that moment when you're rendered completely helpless and a life passes before you, haunting you forever like a video replaying what you think you should've done. Callie, you said, "This is my calling. It's what God wants me to do, and it feels so right."

I need a moment to collect myself, sorry.

And then LT barged in the office. Out of breath, he braced himself with one hand on my desk that had been transformed into our dinner table. He leaned in and spoke in a hushed voice. The sweat from his brow dripped onto my shoulder. "Sorry," he said as he wiped his forehead.

"Carry on," I replied.

"Our team got hit, Sir. QRF is on their way out the gate ... but we're missing the medics. It was their convoy in the blast."

Callie, you popped out of your seat and said, "Tell 'em to pack a kit. I'm going." You ran to the door, paused, looked back at me, and said, "Daddy, I won't disappoint you. Love you." You blew me a kiss and then sprinted to the motor pool before I could say a word.

"Why did you have to do that in front of her, LT?" My fingers tensed in preparation to strangle him. He apologized, stumbling over his words. It was too late; you were long gone.

Part of me was so proud, but most of me was terrified. If anyone could bring my troops back, it'd be you. This wasn't your first rodeo, cowgirl.

I ran to the TOC to further assess the situation. It was bustling, coordinating care and relaying critical information through the chain of command. I took a seat. The room came into sharper focus as my battle mind took over: three vehicles down, nine presumed KIA, and five casualties. No medics on the scene yet. The casualties would have to render buddy care to one another in the interim. Eight minutes until your ETA. The birds were right behind you carrying another team of medics for air evacuation.

Callie, what were you thinking during that ride? Were you strategizing? Rehearsing medical procedures? Did you think of me? Were you scared? Did you pray?

You arrived and I jumped outta my seat to watch you on video. The image was far from high-def, but I knew which hustling body was yours. Your movement and mannerisms were obvious, so quick on your feet. You ran around the site of the mass casualty to orient yourself and your team. You created a game plan and directed the medic to triage casualties in a specific order. Your voice was muffled over the radios, and then it all went silent.

Why did we lose connectivity? "Where are the birds?" I asked LT. As soon as I turned to ask him, bright light radiated from the screen. My heart stopped and my breath escaped me. I ground my feet into the concrete floor, smashing my fist into the wooden desk at my side. The pain reminded me that this was reality—not a nightmare in my cot. You were hit by a command detonated IED meant specifically for you: the first responders. I had to get to you—now.

Please not her, God … not her. Lord, please … keep her safe.… God, I will commit everything to You if You don't take her from me. Please … I was bargaining with God. Like a reflex, I harnessed my weapon on my back, stocked up on medical kits, went straight for the motor pool, and jumped inside the nearest up-armored vehicle.

One thought turned me into a blood-seeking killer.

The MPs saw the "crazy" in my eyes, so they stopped me, dragged me out of the vehicle, and confined me to my office.

I stood at the doorframe in disbelief that you were here just minutes ago. I can't rewind those minutes, but I'd do anything—absolutely anything—if I could.

I ran to the table and pressed my finger into your steak. It was still warm. The plates became flying saucers that exploded against the walls. My hands tore through everything that could be thrown or broken, until I detected my CSM standing at the doorway in my peripheral vision. He cleared his throat. "She's here, but it's critical, brother."

"Take me to her," I commanded.

Terror poured over me. I prepared myself to see you in pieces and drenched in red. The combat support hospital smelled sterile, mixed with the scent of metal … iron … blood. The hallway floor was smeared with prints of red combat boots. I stood at the divider that separated your bed from an Iraqi soldier beside you. Adrenaline surged through me as I pictured myself suffocating him. I pushed the thought back because you needed me first. Everything was in slow motion as I pulled back the curtain. Instantly your eyes caught mine. I refused to let go of your gaze, fearing what I might see if I looked below your face, but I had to. My body went limp and I desperately grabbed at the curtain to keep from falling backward. Only half of you came back to me.

Your eyes opened and closed as you faded in and out of consciousness. I whispered into your ear, but it was barely intact. I grabbed my mouth, fearing I might moan and cause you distress. I forced myself to maintain my bearing and strength for you, darling. I leaned in to kiss your cheek and whispered, "Your daddy loves you, baby girl." Your hand tightened around mine. You heard me. I couldn't hold back the tears that burst from my eyes. Your grip was still firm. "I'm proud of you, Callie—there is no prouder dad than me." Your eyes opened wide and peered into the depths of my soul as a gentle smile spread across your face.

I would've done anything to switch places with you, my dear. The machines began to scream and your smile faded. You looked beyond me as a gentle wave of peace came over you and flowed through me where our hands were intertwined. It was the longest moment of my life, and then your body went limp as the last surge of energy pulsed through you and ended at our touch.

The medical team burst into your cubicle. They worked around your cold, stiffened grip on my hand. They didn't push me away because they knew it was too late.

Sweat poured down your doctor's face as she attempted to revive you via chest compressions. She mourned for me because as your energy left, so did mine. After what felt like eternity, she stopped, exhausted and sobbing. Her eyes locked with mine for a heartbeat. Violently, she pulled her gloves from her hands and threw them on the blood-soaked floor, along with her surgical cap. She avoided my persistent gaze, as she could not confront the emotion of a father who had just lost his daughter in such a horrific way. Her eyes spoke her heart. I wanted to tell her that it wasn't her fault, but my lips couldn't form words. She muttered, "Time of death 0316." She stopped in her tracks, looked at me, and whispered, "John 3:16 ... Where is God?" She wiped the snot from her nose, said, "I'm so sorry," then disappeared down the hall. I sat there, emptier than a drum. My baby girl, who was on her way to save lives, was dead right before my eyes. *Where were You, God?*

As far as I was concerned, there was no God. And you were gone—gone forever, with no hope of a reunion at the pearly white gates of heaven. If there was no God, there was certainly no heaven.

No one recognized me; I didn't recognize myself.

I spent an hour at your bedside until my CSM ripped me away from you. It was time for the medical team to prepare your body for your final flight home. It was goodbye—forever. Sounds of your last breath, your pale face, the contrast of your fierce blue eyes having lost their light, and rows of flag-draped coffins have suffocated my nightmares for years.

Nothing could bring me peace, Callie—absolutely nothing. Anger and rage became second nature. No one recognized me; I didn't recognize myself. I'm grateful you didn't have to see who I became—a calloused man, drained of life. I picked up your rucksack and finished your journey—from one deployment to the next. At full speed, I threw myself into what became *our* military career—no longer mine alone. It was the only thing that kept me alive.

A year later, I convinced behavioral health that I was good to go on another deployment. Of course, I wasn't good to go. I had ulterior motives—a mission for bloodthirsty revenge. But I was able to keep a composed front, forcing that plastic smile that everyone wanted to see, or needed to see. To them, I was the poster child for resilience.

Every deployment, I followed the rules of engagement as liberally as they could be interpreted without breaking them. I became a monster—it's no wonder your mother left me. One deployment passed after another.

In the aftermath of an ambush, an Iraqi father stood grieving over the dead body of his teenage son. Revenge and justice flooded my veins. I allowed myself to find joy in his darkest moment. I stood watching him, transfixed on how his tears gracefully fell into his cupped, prayerful hands. How did he pray so peacefully to a God who had brutally stolen his son? After your death, Callie, God became my enemy.

Two weeks after that firefight, we returned to the same small village to capture an HVT. The first door we kicked in, there he stood—that same father. His face was a paradox. It was gaunt and pale with eyes sunk deep into his skull. But there was something about those eyes—they were bright and alive, like glowing amber. He looked at me calmly, as if he were expecting me. Face to face, he was no longer a distant enemy. My team pulled him outside and pinned him to the ground faster than I could catch my breath. "Stand down," I commanded my team. I grabbed the man's arm to help him up; he dusted off his face, unfazed. Adrenaline coursed through me, and my breath quickened—but his breath was different. It was deep, like that of an old man sitting contented in his rocking chair, staring out at the sunset from his front porch. Everything about his energy was incongruent with ours.

He gently reached out his hand. "I'm Abu Hanny. How can I help you?" he asked in a broken accent.

He spoke English surprisingly well. Eyebrows raised in unison among the green suits that encircled us for my protection. "I remember you," I replied, making the conscious effort to soften my tone. In simple English, I explained that I saw him mourn his son. I told him I was truly sorry for his loss and that I understood his pain because of what happened to you, Callie.

He looked directly at me and abruptly grabbed both of my hands. My body tensed but I grounded myself in the loose sand as the circle of green suits drew nearer to me, shrinking their formation. "I'm sorry, my friend who understands my hurt." I asked him how he could see me as a friend, if my men had killed his son as his people had killed my daughter? He paused me with one finger, as if saying, *Hold that thought.* Then he beckoned us into his home. Three of my Soldiers cleared it before I entered.

It was like any other home in that village—quaint and minimal, made of mud and stone. Elaborate prayer rugs hung on walls. He led us to his kitchen table. Only three chairs—one each for the two of us, plus our interpreter, should I need him.

"We serve the same master," he said. I leaned in to hear him better, as if doing so would help me tune out his thick accent. "But we go about it differently," he continued. "It is our selfish ways that pollute the peace that we should be living in right now. It is we who create this terror—not God." He ran his fingers through his unruly white beard. "It is when our values clash that war begins. It is because we want the treasures of this world more than God." He began to quote from the Quran: "'This because they *love* the life of this world better than the Hereafter: And Allah will not guide those who reject Faith.'" [†]

It made sense. He believed in an eternal life and lived his life on earth in preparation for that.

"Do you grieve for your son?" I asked.

"Of course. But I will see him soon. I wish he had been born in a country like America. Here, no freedom. We are ruled by extremists. Here, we try to survive ... and that means turning our heads to very bad things ... things I pray God forgives me for. You are blessed to live like you do. I imagine your daughter joined the military because of you. She had a choice. My son did not. He was forced to do things he did not believe in, in order to survive, so that I may survive as well. I am grateful that he is now at peace and no longer has to live in fear. I will join him soon."

He stood slowly and approached the stove to pour me a small cup of tea.

"*Shukraan,*" I replied as he handed me the cup. Tears streamed down my face and embarrassment burned my cheeks.

"It is okay, my friend. You will see her again ... and it will be glorious ... the way it was meant to be." His conviction brought him a peace that surpassed understanding. "I will see my son and wife again too. They took her head for teaching girls to read. They will also take mine, but I am ready."

Abu Hanny spent the next few minutes writing on a torn piece of notebook paper. He carefully creased the edges and folded it into a small square. He licked his dried lips and kissed the paper and then handed it to me.

"These men who killed your daughter do not worship the same God I do." He placed his hand on the Quran that sat on the small table.

[†]   Quran 16:107, italics mine.

"That paper is all you need. Pray that our God can forgive me and allow me to join my family."

"Thank you, my friend." I squeezed his shoulder—a gesture of solidarity. Once in the brief embrace, I looked around the room at glossy eyes resisting the fall of tears. Moments later, I extracted my team from his home. Several Soldiers stocked it with water and food, but Abu Hanny rejected it and said there was no use for that now. He requested we give the goods to his neighbor.

I opened the letter upon our return to the vehicles. The interpreter read it aloud. Abu Hanny provided the specific location of the top three HVTs. All correct locations, I might add. He ended the note with one of the ninety-nine Arabic names for God: Al-Wadud (the all-loving and all-forgiving God). This situation turned into the biggest accomplishment of my military career, and I found it to be the most enlightening.

How could I find God and revelation in a place like this?

From that moment on, I praised and thanked God for my eternal life through Christ our Savior. I am undeserving of His grace, love, mercy, and, most importantly, His forgiveness. With my heavenly Father at the center of my life, Father's Day has taken on an entirely new meaning.

In 2009, I chose to pick up your rucksack to continue your legacy until mission complete. Well, my daughter, I'm honored to say that we made it to retirement.

And with that, my dearest Callie, I find peace … until we meet again.

☆ ☆ ☆

Forgiveness

When we refuse to forgive, whether it's directed toward someone else or ourselves, we live in bondage to the Enemy. Directing our unforgiveness toward someone else is like drinking poison and expecting *them* to die from it. It enslaves us to anger and fury. Remember, people who are hurting hurt other people. The Enemy lies to us, telling us we are unworthy of forgiveness and that we should continue to punish ourselves.

But Jesus has compassion for our hurt. When we ask, He forgives us for the wrongs we commit because of our pain. The truth is, doing wrong in our hurting only brings more chaos. Only forgiveness can set us free. Why would we choose the word of the Enemy over the word of God? If God declares we're forgiven, then it's a certainty. The Enemy never wants us to believe that truth because once we forgive ourselves the way God has forgiven us, then we're free to love and be loved. We must be free of the Enemy's lies about forgiveness in order to be vessels of God's love and purpose for our lives. When we're free, we're capable of setting others free through the power of God's love.

To forgive someone who has wronged you does not mean establishing a close relationship with that person. In fact, God wants you to guard your heart from those who have caused you harm (see Prov. 4:23). The purpose of forgiving is to set you free from the negative power your transgressor has over you. The person you forgive may never know that you've forgiven him or her; forgiveness is solely for your own peace of mind. As God has forgiven us, we must also forgive others: "Bear with each other and forgive one another if any of you has a grievance against someone. Forgive as the Lord forgave you." (Col. 3:13). Forgiveness is a demonstration of grace that your transgressor may not deserve, yet you deserve the peace that flows from it.

Part IV

What's Next for You and Your Family?

The emotional impact of our combat experiences on our loved ones, where to go for help, and determining what's next

Chapter 12

COMBAT AND MARRIAGE

Couples Rebuilding Hope Together

The following fictional letter could have been written to James by his wife upon his return from Afghanistan. After chapter 1, James continued to struggle with thoughts of suicide until he finally surrendered to professional and spiritual help.

James,

I can never forgive you. To place a loaded pistol in your mouth in front of me—there's no words for that! I hate you for it. How could you do that to me? You made me wrestle it from your hands, and then made me the bad guy. Am I that awful of a woman to make you want to kill yourself and miss out on the lives of your children? Did you do it to dig the knife deeper into my soul, knowing what my father did when I was a kid? I'll be damned if I see another man's brains sprayed against bedroom walls. My dad said he hated his life because of me, and then you did that?

Truthfully, I hate you most days, but I love you. I don't know who you are anymore. You're not the man I married—not even close. There's no resemblance to the old you—goofy, tender, and in love with me—pushing me to go to church when I didn't believe.

In all your bullsh**, I've lost myself. Who am I? I don't like the new me, much like you seem to despise yourself and everyone else. You suffocate me with your anger. This evil is contagious, and like a cancer it's spreading to our children. They're helpless, and I'm hopeless.

You shut me down every time I try to talk to you about us. I give up! You yell, open another bottle, and disappear into the black hole. I hate that garage. I wish I could set fire to it! It's sucked you in, and now you never come out.

I'm hurting more than I've ever hurt before. I keep asking myself, *How much longer can I tolerate this? Where are You, God? Help me!*

The Army calls me your dependent. That's all I am—dependent on you in every aspect of my existence—and I hate it! My daily mood depends on you. Did you know that you make or break me if you don't kiss me goodbye in the mornings? I pretend to be asleep, but each day it's a test: Am I worthy or not? You've become a damn zombie, but I'd rather have a hug from a zombie when you return from work than none at all.

Don't be surprised that I feel this way. I'm desperate to have you back. When I run from you, I run to church, something I never thought I'd do in a million years. Nor did I ever imagine sitting alone through the service. Now that I'm a believer, you couldn't care less …

I'm embarrassed to even think this or let it escape my mouth. But damn, do I have PTSD? You may think it's stupid, and you may get pissed—well, you're always pissed—but I feel traumatized even though I'm not the combat vet. But you will never understand how f'd-up it is to be completely helpless while you're a billion miles away at war with a target on your head! I was a damn news junkie; everything they broadcast sent me into a state of panic. Every day my heart raced as my mind took me down to terrible places. If the doorbell rang, I lost my sh**, thinking it was the Chaplain coming.

I obsessed over video footage of combat and visualized you bleeding out. My dreams were saturated in blood and explosions to the point that I had to detach myself from all emotions. Every time my phone rang, my heart blasted from my chest fearing it was bad news. Some days, I pretended that you were already dead to desensitize me from the possibility of it. Has that pushed me away from you?

Do you even care that I've been a single parent for years now? It sucks. I didn't sign up for that. Not only are you gone during deployments, but you're emotionally absent 24-7-365. I was supposed to go to nursing school, remember? I saw more for my life than just this! I've sacrificed everything for you. You can't even say "thank you" because everything with you is "woe is me." Being a combat vet is your cop-out for everything! I'm sick of your sob story.

I'm sorry for being this raw. This letter wasn't meant to get you to put a pistol in your mouth again, I promise. This letter, just a mere sheet of paper, is the weight of all my hurt and suffering.

I get it! This deployment wasn't our first, but this sh** doesn't get any easier; it gets harder. Each deployment you survive, I tell myself, *Well, he escaped death this time around; it's coming the next time …* The funny thing is, you're already dead. Better yet, we're already dead. Does it even matter at this point? God help us!

Love you mostly!
Vero

Before couple's therapy began, James pursued individual therapy with another counselor. He had to work through his own issues before he was emotionally ready to integrate his wife into his recovery. James was overwhelmed with shame, so he built a fortress around his heart that only the Holy Spirit could break through. After this realization, he began to see the truth, and his freedom was finally in sight. He learned who God really is and how the Enemy was prevailing in the spiritual battle for his soul. He recognized that it had to stop. Finally, he was receptive to his wife's feedback and ready to choose truth over the Enemy's deception.

He had to work through his own issues before he was emotionally ready to integrate his wife into his recovery.

His counselor used Rhythm Restoration to help James see the presence of God throughout his life and his hellish deployments. He was able to make peace with Carl, his best friend who bled out in his arms in Iraq. James blamed himself for Carl's death but was set free from the twisted guilt of the Enemy when he visualized his friend's heavenly existence. Speaking the truth about Carl's death terrified James, but during an RR session, Carl expressed his love for James and gave him permission to live free. Now it was time for James and Veronica to find their peace.

First Couple's Session

We prayed for truth and healing to prevail before we began exploring the walls Veronica and James had carefully constructed around their hearts. Twirling her long black hair around and around her finger, Veronica sat at the opposite end of the sofa from James. He sat hunched and nearly swallowed by an oversized Army hoodie that enveloped his way-too-short buzz cut.

To start, I instructed the couple to sit closer in two chairs, facing each other almost knee to knee. James grunted like a teenager, demonstrating his discomfort at being so close to his wife, and Veronica rolled her eyes in response. This exchange accurately represented the great wall they had built between them.

"Veronica. James," I said sternly as my eyes darted back and forth between them. "Imagine this: The Father, the Son, and the Holy Spirit are sitting together at a table, talking and laughing with one another. A man approaches and asks, 'Which one of You is the boss?' But before They can respond, the man points to the Father and says, 'I bet You're the head honcho.' All three laugh and at the same time respond, 'We're in perfect surrender to one another.' The Father explains, 'That's the problem with My children. They focus so much on power, control, and hierarchy that they miss out on relationship and love. They miss out on the purpose of their creation.'" I rolled my chair in closer and asked, "Do you see how by focusing on power dynamics, you're missing out on relationship with each other? Can you both surrender to each other today?"

"Yes," said James. We were surprised that he chimed in first. James reached for Veronica's hand, and a tear escaped from under her black lashes. Veronica's eyes locked on his, and she replied, "I surrender to you.... It's my last resort."

Veronica's free hand trembled as she clutched tightly to the letter she had written to James (above). She began to read it out loud. As her words formed sentences, the past walls she had so carefully constructed began to break away in the presence of truth. When James squeezed her hand, a stray tear turned into a waterfall, halting her delivery. For the first time, Veronica's words didn't fall on deaf ears.

James hunched over, sobbing, as her words sank in. He allowed himself to feel the depth of her pain.

When she finished reading, she embraced James and said, "This letter doesn't account for all the hurt I know I caused you. I was never perfect throughout any of this."

"James, is there a big truth you want to share with Veronica today?" I asked. They were learning that the Enemy uses the perception of offense to justify causing one another more pain. As the saying goes, "Hurt people hurt people," and this vicious cycle can only be stopped when we choose communication over vengeance and defense.

"Yes." James wrapped his arms tightly around his midsection as he rocked back and forth. "I blamed myself for Carl's death." The weight of those words caused James to collapse onto Veronica's lap. He whispered, "I'm so sorry. I wish it were me who died that day." James continued to whisper, "I'm so sorry. Forgive me. Forgive me. Forgive me."

Veronica ran her fingers through his short hair as tears fell from her face onto him. "It's not your fault, James. I know you would take a bullet for any of your Marines!" She wiped the tears from his eyes. "What happened?" she asked softly.

After about a minute, James lifted his head, his eyes met hers, and he told her how their convoy had slept on the road that night. After only four hours of alternating between watch and sleep, the unit was abruptly awakened to a new set of orders. The team was "groggy and pissed" as they readied themselves for their new mission and ate a quick breakfast in their vehicles as they rolled out. Distracted by their food and operating in the poor light of dusk, no one noticed the shade of the asphalt change from light to dark gray. Covered by fresh asphalt, an IED and pressure plate had just been laid. James blamed himself because, sitting atop the tanker, he believed he had the best view and it should've been evident to him.

"Veronica, Carl died in my arms," he exclaimed. "I felt his last breath on my face and his warm blood all over my hands. I can still feel it now!" They folded into each other in deep catharsis. He sat up, took her face in his hands, and said, "I couldn't tell you because I wanted to be your hero, but I've failed miserably in every way. Holding this back from you turned me into a monster. I'm sorry."

When James failed to recognize God's presence, it was because he was too busy looking down and focusing on his sorrow rather than looking up at his loving Father.

With her face still embraced, Veronica placed her hands over his and replied, "You're still my hero. I'm sorry you felt like you had to walk through hell alone. But I thank God that He was with you and led us here." The couple embraced, and Veronica whispered in his ear, "It's not your fault. Carl wouldn't want you to blame yourself."

The deep shame that James harbored caused him to withdraw from Veronica and everyone he loved. He felt unworthy of any good. The Enemy clung to every negative emotion and belief to deceive James, causing him to separate himself from the many facets of God's love. Once he acknowledged his truth, Veronica was able to empathize with his hurt and suffering. She demonstrated judgment-free love, the kind of love that God exudes. United, James and Veronica recognized their incredible potential to advance the kingdom of God, and with that, they understood that the Enemy would aim to divide and conquer them.

Couple's Therapy and Rhythm Restoration

In our first couple's iteration of Rhythm Restoration, I took Veronica and James back to a dark place: the night she found him with a loaded pistol in his mouth. I encouraged them to fully immerse themselves in the memory. After processing, they looked up and shook their heads in disbelief, as if the event had happened many years ago and not just recently. "I can't believe that happened," Veronica said. "I don't like what I saw or who I was." She squeezed James's hand.

In our next iteration of RR, I asked them to visualize switching roles. Veronica imagined she was James in the intense moment of his suicide attempt, and vice versa. Tears poured down their faces because, for the first time, they truly understood each other's hurt and pain. Apologies poured from their lips as they recognized the many ways they had fallen for the Enemy's traps. From twisted guilt to self-righteousness and offense, they continually added fuel to the fire of hurt.

James expressed his deep regret not only for his decision to attempt suicide but especially for the manner he chose. In the midst of his hurting, he hadn't recognized how his behavior took Veronica back to when she was a nine-year-old girl walking into the gruesome scene of her father's horrific death. All this time, she thought James had reenacted this scene to intentionally hurt her. But as they surrendered to each other, the truth was revealed, and they recognized they had been badly deceived by the Enemy.

Applying this technique of role reversal in RR also allowed for the couple to gain insight into each other's struggles during James's deployment. He realized how difficult it was for Veronica to feel helpless and terrified of losing him on a daily basis. He noted that it was probably more emotionally draining for her than for him.

Blocking their suffering may have worked well temporarily, but with it they also blocked out the potential for experiencing positive emotions, like love and the opportunity for healing. If we choose pride and self-righteousness over surrender, how often do these walls remain an obstacle forever?

God for Us

I asked Veronica and James to visualize how God had been present with them throughout their last deployment experience. Veronica smiled and said, "He brought me to the church, my salvation—something you always aspired to for me, James."

He took a deep breath, looked up, and said, "Thank You, Jesus."

Crossing her arms and looking into the distance, Veronica appeared to be deep in thought. "James, this deployment was hell on me, but that hell forced me to take refuge in Jesus, which in turn was the greatest blessing," she said, placing her hands on her heart. "Our Lord put all the right people in my life at the right time. During every emergency I had in your absence, God brought resolution to it. And the way He used others to help me was nothing shy of a miracle. In that same way, we're going to be a blessing to Carl's wife as an extension of God's love for her."

"Yes, we will be," said James as he slid closer to his wife. "And I'm so sorry that I didn't show my appreciation and happiness for your salvation." He placed his hand on her leg. "Since I lost Carl, I stopped believing in God because I thought He was the one responsible for his death. I didn't want you to get hurt by God too—I was so lost—but now I understand the truth. If it's not love, it's not God." James buried his head in his hands and then quickly wiped the tears from his face. "I'm so grateful to finally share my faith with you. I'm no longer going to allow the Enemy to steal and destroy all the blessings God has given me—us."

James explained that during the hardest time of his life, he felt the presence of God in the love and brotherhood of his Marines. He found God when interacting with the Iraqi children on "heart and mind" missions. He literally found God in a foxhole during a firefight. God saved his life every time someone intervened during his suicide attempts. James saw clearly that God never left him. When James failed to recognize God's presence, it was because he was too busy looking down and focusing on his sorrow rather than looking up at his loving Father.

During another Rhythm Restoration visualization, I asked James and Veronica to see each other through the eyes of God. In that image, I instructed them to view their spouse with the crown of life and the full armor of God (see Rev. 2:10; Eph. 6:10–18). Both of them smiled wide, and Veronica broke out into laughter.

This time, she wiped happy tears from her cheeks and said, "James, Jesus loves you more than you can possibly imagine. I saw Him place a crown of antlers on your head, and you wore camouflage, of course! He knows how much you love hunting! You looked like a frickin' moose!" She laughed and continued, "Jesus told me that it's your job to continue hunting, but this time you are to hunt men for the purpose of bringing them to Christ."

James laughed, cried, and blew snot all at the same time. "My turn," he replied. "You looked gorgeous. You wore a crown of pearls and your armor was pearl white."

Veronica's eyes widened, and she looked down at the pearl engagement ring James had given her over a decade ago.

James went on, "God told me that you're like a pearl: a beautiful creation that came from tremendous hurt and pain. Just as an oyster creates a pearl to mend the hurt caused by a grain of sand, you've made beauty from your suffering. You also mend the minds and bodies of many, and someday you'll become a healer—a nurse or doctor. It's your destiny to serve our Lord in that way, and I'll make sure you stay on His path to fulfill it."

They embraced and together visualized their future surrendering to God. That day, they learned Ecclesiastes 4:12: "Though one may be overpowered, two can defend themselves. A cord of three strands is not quickly broken." By surrendering and choosing life, they learned that the Holy Spirit is the source and strength of their marriage—the missing piece—the third cord.

Families, please remember, life and death are in the power of the tongue, so choose life (see Prov. 18:21). Whatever you point out in your spouse or children is guaranteed to produce. If all you focus on is their flaws, you will get more of their flaws. But if you acknowledge their good, you will get more of their good. A simple "I believe in you" produces life and inspires growth. Whether it's your thoughts, your actions, or your words, choose life and let them be of love.

Chapter 13

FINAL THOUGHTS AND YOUR BIG QUESTIONS

You made it to the end, but even with all you've read, you may still have some big questions about your experiences, healing from combat, and the way forward. It's my hope that this final chapter will close that gap and bring peace to your incredible journey ahead.

Why Do We Have to Play Fair? The Enemy Doesn't—Not Even Close.

The military rules of engagement are the rules or directives among military forces (including individuals) that define the circumstances, conditions, degree, and manner in which the use of force, or actions which might be construed as provocative, may be applied. Rules of engagement do not normally dictate how a result is to be achieved but will indicate what measures may be unacceptable. Essentially, the rules of engagement are a moral compass that clarifies the boundaries of fighting in a war.

God's Rules of Engagement

> Do to others as you would have them do to you.
> (Luke 6:31)

Where there is no vision, the people are unrestrained, but happy is the one who keeps the Law. (Prov. 29:18 NASB)

Blessed are they who observe justice, who do righteousness at all times! (Ps. 106:3 ESV)

If your enemy is hungry, feed him; if he is thirsty, give him something to drink; for by so doing you will heap burning coals on his head. (Rom. 12:20 ESV)

On the other hand, God favors those who trust in Him and seek to fight for just reasons. He acknowledges that there is a time for war and a time for peace. When the time for war comes, He commands us to fight with fairness and to show compassion for the enemy. God instructs us to refrain from taking revenge, as bringing justice is His duty—not ours. We fight fair because we obey His command, and in doing so, we are blessed. In His kingdom, we're to follow His Word and goodness will prevail. Sometimes it's difficult to comprehend that goodness doesn't always mean earthly good, which we expect in our limited understanding. Sometimes it means spiritual good, and sometimes it's both. Regardless, everything good comes from the Father of lights (see James 1:17).

Why fight fair? Because when you sow a bad seed, sooner or later it will produce, and what you reap will be equally bad—or even worse. Everything produces after its own kind. This includes your thoughts and actions. If you commit war crimes or seek revenge, you will produce negativity within your own life—whether the consequences are physical, emotional, or spiritual. Hurt will only beget more hurt; don't be the source of unnecessary suffering.

Remember, the Enemy doesn't want you to have God's favor. The Enemy wants to provoke you to fight unfairly, take revenge, and become a lawless savage. The Enemy wants to plant the seed of hatred in your mind. The Enemy wants you to water it so that the seed of emotional pain can flourish like a weed, sucking the life from everything you love until, finally, its destruction torments you to the point of suicide. The Enemy delights in winning the physical war but takes the greatest satisfaction in winning the emotional and spiritual war.

How Can My Family Help Me?

Oddly enough, the return from deployment transition can be more difficult than gearing up to deploy, as you must confront the over-stimulation, the family void, the hype, and worst of all, the expectation that you'll be the same ol' you. Let's face it, that's not likely going to happen. You probably feel angry, irritable, emotionally disconnected, overwhelmed, and hypervigilant. All of this will make you want to take cover in your man/woman cave, which will undoubtedly irritate your family, since they haven't seen you in what feels like forever. Their disappointment and frustration will likely exacerbate your anger, until a divide forms from the failed expectations, poor communication, and lack of understanding. You may feel like you can't do anything right by your loved ones, so you give up and feel sorry for yourself. And before you know it, your family becomes your adversary.

Warrior: Don't keep your

family in the dark.

Warning: this may come across as harsh, but we've come this far, so let me speak the truth. Just because you had an awful combat deployment doesn't mean your family must tiptoe around you. They should be considerate, but they shouldn't change who they are to accommodate you. Let's cut to the chase: the sooner you stop feeling sorry for yourself at home, the sooner you'll find peace with your new normal.

Many of my Soldiers express feeling as though they've been "victims" of war. As a result, they feel a sense of entitlement to behave a certain way upon returning home. Yes, I'm referring to excessive outbursts of anger, irritability, and chronic self-isolation, often accompanied by heavy substance use. I get it. I do. It's not unusual to feel this way. But acting like a jerk will just complicate everything!

Try your best to override your emotions by accessing your powerful thoughts and making them captive to Christ; your family deserves the best of you. The choice to feel like a victim of war is yours, just like the choice to join the military was yours. You chose to deploy, knowing the risks. The bottom line is this: the sooner you hold yourself accountable for your actions, the sooner you and your family will begin to heal.

Family: Please be patient and understand that it isn't you. It's important to validate your warrior's emotional experience and encourage him or her to seek help. In addition to reading this book, learn about PTSD and what treatment looks like. Accompany your loved one to his or her first treatment session and share your concerns with your warrior's therapist. I highly recommend family therapy with a clinician who truly understands how to work with warriors experiencing posttraumatic stress.

When your warrior finally decides to disclose to you "what happened" (which I highly recommend), be open and receptive. *Do not* be judgmental or criticize his experience. Your warrior is taking a big risk to open up and become vulnerable about what could possibly be the most painful experience of his life. Do *not* place blame on him or say "That's it?" You don't want your loved one to shut down and leave you out of his healing process, as that will have a terrible impact on your family dynamic.

Family: Don't let the Enemy establish a war zone in your home.

Warrior: Don't keep your family in the dark. They're not as fragile as you think. I assure you they're probably already imagining the worst-case scenario about what you've experienced to prepare their minds for the worst. If you wish to disclose your experience to your loved ones, you can dedicate one of your therapy sessions to doing so with the gentle guidance of your therapist. First, start with your significant other and then determine which children (being mindful of their ages) or family members are ready and would benefit from more information to better understand why you may be struggling.

Family: Don't let the Enemy establish a war zone in your home. Your warrior isn't the only one diligently serving our country. You're the reason she is able to serve in the capacity she does. We recognize your dedication and perseverance as a significant source of her strength. You're the bow and she's the arrow. Without you, she doesn't fly as far, as fast, or as accurately. Without you, her mission isn't complete.

Healing: A Force Multiplier

Returning to the fight with a healthy heart and mind helps you to identify others in need of healing. If you had the courage to heal (through Christ), then others can too. Now that you know the process, you can clarify any misconceptions that many military members have about behavioral health.

Your behavioral health clinic on post/base, Veterans Affairs (VA), or vet center may be the best place to start healing. Don't believe the lies: you won't be kicked out of the military for seeking help! The goal is your emotional healing so you can get back into the fight. You and your therapist will talk about your best options and how you feel about your mission capabilities. All efforts are to help you get better as soon as possible.

The most common methods are individual and group therapy, as well as psychotropic medication management. Medical discharge from a behavioral health perspective is fairly uncommon; most Soldiers return to duty—which is great news! Medical discharge only occurs when one's providers have exhausted most options with no treatment success and deem it best that the Service Member continue to focus on healing without concern of ever deploying again.

Remember, you must fill your cup first in order to keep pouring out for others. Take care of yourself—emotionally, physically, and spiritually.

Can I Return to the Fight?

Of course you can! But are you ready? Have you made peace with the past so you can move forward? Picture this: The hurt and pain of a traumatic event starts off the size of a snowball. You could crush that snowball immediately by emotionally digesting the impact of the event on your life. However, like a snowball rolling downhill, which grows larger and larger until it becomes an avalanche, your traumatic life event will also compound with other events if you ignore it, until it becomes like an avalanche of pain and dysfunction overtaking your life. Remember, avoidance is the hallmark symptom of PTSD.

Do you feel capable of going back into combat? Do you feel confident that you will enhance your team's overall mission completion? If not, then I suggest you focus on receiving treatment until you're ready. You may also decide it's not worth it to deploy again—especially in light of all the effort it took for both you and your family to recover from your last deployment. There is no one correct answer. Everyone processes trauma differently. I encourage you to seek professional guidance to help answer these critical questions while including your family in the decision-making process. Of course, pray for the Lord's guidance when making this life decision.

The most important thing is that you make peace with your decision. There is no shame in not returning to the fight, and many combat veterans have made this choice. Sometimes it takes more courage to say no. Remember, the military doesn't skip a beat. The crucial role you once played in the fabric of your unit will quickly be closed and mended in your absence. Don't be offended by the nature of the beast.

The battle you fought both physically and spiritually was a great sacrifice, and that's enough. *You are enough.* Remember, freedom isn't free. You fought long and hard for it in combat. Above all else, never forget that your ultimate freedom came from the cross that our Lord and Savior carried for you and eventually died on for your salvation.

☆ ☆ ☆

A vessel can only do two things: pour out and be poured into. Your vessel may be psychologically and spiritually clogged from the hurt of your past. However, I hope what you've learned in this book will help to unclog your vessel so that you may be poured into again and eventually allow yourself to pour out love to those around you.

I also pray that the combat veteran testimonies in this book inspire you to have hope and faith for a better future—one filled with peace, purpose, and above all else, love. What you've learned about your experiences as you've read will not only be of service to you but will allow you to be a force multiplier, helping your fellow brothers and sisters in need. Teaching someone about a simple topic, such as explaining twisted guilt, can help him reframe his entire traumatic experience and bring peace to his story. Reading someone the poem "If They Could Speak" (found in chapter 4) can return life and love to a space where only death and anger existed.

You don't need to be a doctor of psychology to bring healing to a fellow combat veteran. It's simple: be a vessel of God's love, and He will guide you to say the right thing at the right time. Professional help is great, but do not underestimate the power of God within you to bring about healing. For most, there's nothing like talking to a brother- or sister-in-arms who has a testimony about a similar emotional experience as yours. We are meant to do this together!

Once you've found your peace after combat, allow yourself to be a vessel of God's love for those who've suffered in similar ways. Remember, you're not alone—nor have you ever been alone; God has always been and will always be on your side.

ADDITIONAL INFORMATION

Here are some ways to support our military, veterans, and their families:

1. Be considerate of our veterans' combat experiences. If you bring up the topic of their careers or their deployment experiences, be aware of potentially triggering the painful memories that they may still be processing. If you are interested in learning about their "war stories," first ask permission to address the topic. Be sensitive to their responses, and afford them the privacy to decline further discussion of the topic. Please, never abruptly ask, "How many bad guys did you kill?" Believe it or not, this question is quite frequently blurted out. It is imperative to be sensitive to experiences that are deeply personal and spiritual.

2. Most Service Members enjoy receiving care packages from their friends and family. If you feel inclined to put a smile on a service member's face, consider putting a box of goodies together and shipping it to his or her deployment location. Be sure to carefully record all the details of the shipping address and ask about any restrictions. Care packages are a great way to boost morale!

3. If you know a family who has sent their loved one off on a deployment, check in on them and ask how you can be of support.

4. When a Service Member returns from deployment, let her know you look forward to seeing her *after* she has settled into the rhythm of home life. Place the ball in her court for having a reunion, as she may need time to physically, psychologically, and emotionally decompress.

5. Learn the difference between Memorial Day and Veterans Day. Memorial Day (the last Monday in May) is when we honor the men and women who have died while serving in the US military. This is traditionally a very somber day for those who serve. It is not the time to thank military members for their service. In contrast, Veterans Day (November 11) is when we show gratitude and appreciation to those who have served our country in war or peace. The differences between the two holidays are important to our veterans.

6. Generously donate to organizations that support Service Members, veterans, and their families. There are many helpful nonprofit organizations that provide a wide range of services to positively impact the lives of those who have made sacrifices in service to our country.

7. Last, if you'd like more information about Rhythm Restoration and my work with combat veterans, I invite you to visit my website at DrTiffanyTajiri.com.

GLOSSARY

1SGT—first sergeant

ACU—Army Combat Uniform

battle rattle—full combat gear that Soldiers wear

battle space—anywhere a mission is executed

block leave—a time when most of a unit takes leave at the same time

BLUF—bottom line up front

cadre—a group or member of a group of leaders, especially in units that conduct formal training schools

Capt.—abbreviation for captain in the US Marine Corps, US Air Force, US Navy, and US Space Force

ChemLight—emergency light stick

COL—colonel

CPT—captain in the US Army

C-RAM—Counter-Rocket, Artillery, Mortar system

CSH—combat support hospital

CSM—command sergeant major

DFAC—dining facility

ETA—estimated time of arrival

FOB—forward operating base

garrison—a military post, often on US soil

green-suiter—an Army officer wearing the green Class A uniform

HVT—high-value target

IED—improvised explosive device

Joes—generic term for Soldiers, typically the junior enlisted personnel

KIA—killed in action

LT—lieutenant

MAJ—major

MEPS—military entrance processing station

motor pool—group of military vehicles

MP—military police

MRE—Meals, Ready-to-Eat

NCO—noncommissioned officer

NDE—near-death experience

PJs—pararescue jumpers

PT clothes—physical training uniforms

PTSD—posttraumatic stress disorder

QRF—quick reaction force redeploy—to relocate personnel

RPG—rocket-propelled grenade

rucking—walking with a loaded backpack

Sandbox, the—a deployment usually to southwest Asia or the Middle East

"See one, do one, teach one"—a method of teaching in which the
    trainee observes a procedure, performs the procedure, and then
    teaches another trainee how to conduct the procedure

SF—Special Forces

SFC—sergeant first class

SGT—sergeant

SPC—specialist

SrA—senior airman

SSgt—staff sergeant

TIC—troops in contact

TOC—tactical operations center

TSgt—technical sergeant

T-wall—a twelve-foot-tall portable, steel-reinforced concrete blast wall

VA—Veterans Affairs

zero dark thirty—early-morning predawn